Teaching Sunday School

Teaching Sunday School

Brian Freer

EP ——————————— EVANGELICAL PRESS

EVANGELICAL PRESS
16—18 High Street, Welwyn, Hertfordshire,
AL6 9EQ, England.

© Evangelical Press 1984

First published 1984
Second Impression 1986

ISBN 0 85234 191 1

Unless otherwise stated, all Bible quotations are from the
New International Version (Hodder & Stoughton 1979)

Typeset in Great Britain by Beaver Reprographics Ltd,
Watford, Herts.
Printed by Anchor Brendon Ltd., Tiptree, Colchester,
England.

Contents

Preface

This little book is not so much a creation as the result of an evolutionary process. It is the result of the author's involvement with children, both as a professional teacher and as a minister concerned with Sunday School work, holiday clubs and the production of Sunday School materials over a period of more than twenty years.

It was the lack of take-home leaflets in connection with the *Go Teach* Sunday School lesson books, originally produced by the F.I.E.C. and now produced by Go Teach Publications, which first caused the author to become involved. Being naive, he enquired about the lack of such take-home leaflets. Very shortly afterwards he found himself incorporated in the publication team with the responsibility of producing these very leaflets! This led him to work in close connection with those responsible for the teaching booklets. The subject of a handbook to help in the training of Sunday School teachers was often discussed. Occasionally meetings were held in connection with one church or another for the purpose of instructing teachers about the conduct of Sunday School and methods of teaching. Each member of that team, therefore, has had some input to this book. Notes borrowed and reworked and woven into a series of talks given over the years have finally evolved into this book.

All things that have evolved must be capable of future evolution. These chapters are not presented as if they were the last word and it is hoped that Sunday School superintendents and ministers may find the book helpful and stimulating to the work of their own Sunday Schools. It is offered with the simple desire that teachers may be helped and encouraged in a task which is so often hard, unrewarding and seemingly never-ending, and if by a perusal of these pages any teacher feels better equipped, delivered from the temptation to give up, or called to work for the Lord in the great mission-field of the children of our land, many of whom grow up in total ignorance of the gospel, then it will have achieved its purpose.

Brian Freer
September 1984

Introduction

The aim of this book is, firstly, to present to the Sunday School teacher a biblical basis for the work he or she does, and, secondly, to establish some basic and guiding principles, so that

1. All the staff (both present and future) will work with the same clear aim in mind;

2. Each teacher will be able to encourage and stimulate others to be diligent in the work;

3. Prospective teachers will become acquainted with all that is involved in Sunday School teaching before they commit themselves to the task;

4. The work of the whole Sunday School can be integrated and structured for the best effect upon the lives of the children.

In order to accomplish these aims, we shall first consider the principles involved in Sunday School teaching and then proceed to examine a number of practical issues, covering the teacher's qualifications, aims and work, the needs of the child, the use of teaching aids and the preparation and presentation of the lesson, in the context of the whole Sunday School period. We shall also summarize the basic content of the gospel we are aiming to present in Sunday School. Finally, we shall consider briefly whether the traditional Sunday School is necessarily the best time and place to reach the children of our day.

For the sake of convenience, teachers and pupils are normally referred to in the masculine gender. Unless the context clearly indicates to the contrary, all remarks apply equally to both male and female teachers and children.

Part 1
Sunday School: the principles

1.
Why Sunday School?—The biblical basis

The question raised

The Sabbath School was introduced by Robert Raikes in 1780. His school differed greatly from the modern concept of a Sunday School. Raikes' aim was to bring literacy to the uneducated, as well as moral and religious teaching. His motive was philanthropic rather than evangelistic. For this reason there are those who seriously oppose the modern practice of teaching children in the Sunday School. Their opposition is based upon convictions about the emphases of Scripture and the practice of earlier Christian generations, notably the Puritans.

Firstly, there is the conviction that the duty to train children is placed by Scripture upon the parents alone (Deut. 6:6-9; Eph. 6:4). It must be said immediately that if the development of the Sunday School has caused Christian parents to abdicate their responsibility in this respect, then there is room for criticism. However, this ought to be directed not against the Sunday School, but against the parents concerned. The laziness and irresponsibility of Christian parents, their sinfulness even, in not availing themselves of their God-given opportunities towards their children, should not be advanced as an argument against

13

Sunday School. The latter simply aims to reinforce in a different way the teaching given by Christian parents, and to supply an opportunity for other children who would otherwise be deprived of such teaching to be instructed in the truths of the Christian faith.

Secondly, there is a conviction, borne of good biblical principles, that children should not be withdrawn from the preaching of the Word. Preaching is God's declared means of saving men. As the malady is identical in the child and in the adult, so the gospel is the same for children as for adults, and its method of proclamation is the same. The children of believers, and others, too, ought to be trained and encouraged to sit under the preaching of the Word. The argument that the sermons are too hard or too long really misses the point. Of course, children will not listen to a whole sermon, but they will get something and if the parents persevere with them they will get more. This is not to say that there will not be difficulties, or that children will always be attentive. It is one of the most inexplicable and extraordinary traits of modern evangelical parents that they seem to have surrendered their authority to the 'wants' and 'don't wants' of their children. The result is that children very often are not 'trained up in the way' at all, but simply left to a choice that they are capable neither of understanding nor of making. Children prefer the security of having choices they do not understand made for them. These matters are particularly important when it comes to the place of children in worship. The children must not be allowed to dictate. There are some families whose whole habit of attendance and choice of place of worship have been unduly influenced by undisciplined children. The secret is to begin early. The inculcation of good habits precludes much of the need for persuasion later on.

There are, of course, difficulties of another kind. We must be in favour of children remaining in the service. The only exception to this is when they become a source of disturbance. A child that is making a disturbance is neither himself profiting nor being trained, nor are the parents profiting because of their distraction, nor is the rest of the congregation profiting. The preacher certainly is not being helped! The insistence on keeping children in the service under such conditions is unintelligent. We must not press our scruples to the point of making them into 'shibboleths' to be defended at all costs.

With regard to the Sunday School, however, we are not considering alternatives. The question is not whether we should teach our own children or send them to Sunday School, whether they should hear the preaching or be taught by a Sunday School teacher, but whether the Sunday School has a complementary function to perform for our own children and a vital service to perform for the children of others. It is surely well within the spirit of the Scriptures (a *spirit* exemplified by the innovation of 'the lecture' by the Puritans when they were prevented from preaching on a Sunday, and later by the introduction of the Sunday School), to use every legitimate means of teaching those who would otherwise not receive a training in the truths of the Bible. Who can seriously oppose such an effort? In all conscience, we are losing the battle for the minds of our children and any effort to counter the godless influences that are forming their minds and attitudes deserves our earnest prayer and encouragement.

Pragmatically therefore the value of the Sunday School can hardly be questioned. But we turn now to examine the biblical principles. Sunday Schools can be justified on the biblical grounds set out in the following paragraphs.

The biblical principles

1. The Great Commission

Every Christian is vitally involved in the Great Commission (Mark 16:15, 16; Matt. 28:18-20). The commission was given to the church as a whole: to the apostles, to evangelists, to missionaries, to pastors and teachers – in fact, to everyone. The command is not so much to '*go* into all the world' as 'As you are going about in all the world, *preach* . . .' It is the command of the risen Lord to every Christian in his daily life to share the gospel with his neighbour. We have a debt of love: 'For Christ's love compels us.' Moreover, if we have any gift, any talent, we are to use it in the building of Christ's church. For these talents and their exercise we are accountable to the Lord. As the command is to preach the gospel to every creature, we may take it that children are included. Children are creatures. Surely the tenderness of our Lord towards the children he encountered in the Gospels puts beyond question our responsibility to them. The negative statement, 'Do not hinder the little children . . .,' surely implies the positive: 'Do all you can to bring them to me.' If the Sunday School is a way of bringing the gospel to 'pagan' children and of reinforcing parental teaching to our own children, then we have the clearest warrant of the Great Commission to use it for teaching purposes.

2. The informal activity of the New Testament church

At a lower level than the formal teaching offices of the New Testament, a great deal of teaching and exhorting went on in the primitive church. Parents are exhorted to train the children (Deut. 6:6,7; Eph. 6:4). Older widows are encouraged to train the younger women (Titus 2:4). Indeed, all believers are encouraged to teach and admonish one another

(Col. 3:16). We believe in the priesthood of all believers and this involves the notion that, in varying degrees, every Christian will have some ability to share his faith with others. It is from this subsoil of informal activity that teaching gifts begin to emerge and are recognized by the church. Some of these develop fully into the pastoral and teaching office. But there are gifts of differing kinds and varying degrees. Thus the informal activity to be observed in the New Testament epistles suggests that a great deal of teaching took place within the local church. It seems justifiable therefore to suggest that this activity may sometimes be organized for the benefit of children.

2.
Spiritual experience and the child

The state of the child

Several things need to be noted:

1. Children do not come straight from heaven with angelic innocence as a built-in advantage. They are 'of the earth', earthy. We are all born 'dead in . . . transgressions and sins,' (Ps. 51:5; Eph. 2:1-3). Even infants, who have not sinned in the same way that Adam sinned, have Adam's sin imputed to them (Rom. 5:14). Thus they are subject to death as the penalty of sin and must be considered sinners (Rom. 5:12-21). The question of the salvation of children, or babies, before the 'age of accountability' is not under consideration here. Our point is that children who can hear and understand the gospel need to hear it, for it is the only remedy for the condition of their sinful souls. The only method of salvation which we know is that revealed in the truths of the Christian faith.

2. Young children are capable of spiritual awareness and are spiritually accountable (2 Tim. 3:14,15; 2 Kings 5:3). Not only so, but the Lord Jesus Christ himself commended the childlike, trusting spirit as the only possible attitude in which a man may enter the kingdom of heaven (Matt. 18:1-5). As the servants of the gospel we have a debt to

children. We owe them a welcome to the kingdom in Christ's name.

3.   The children of our generation are not merely ignorant of the way of salvation; they are largely spiritually unaware. The 'Religious Instruction' received in day school is, for the vast majority, very far removed from the evangelical truths of the Scriptures. The children of today belong to a generation which is ignorant of spiritual matters, as perhaps no other generation since the Reformation has been. The image of God, albeit marred by the Fall, is in them, but they are ignorant of the fact and do not know that they were created as living souls. In the whole ethos governing their existence and education they are regarded merely as highly developed animals. The psychological assumptions behind their whole development overlook the spiritual. We have a vast responsibility to arouse their spiritual awareness as early as we possibly can, and to provide them with the information they need to understand the strivings, questionings and dissatisfactions which stir deep inside them.

4.   Spiritually, the children of our generation are uncared for. Parents, the state, day school teachers, all follow in the steps of those disciples who tried to prevent the children from coming to Jesus. It almost seems to be a Satanically inspired conspiracy. Our schools are rapidly becoming spiritual slaughter-houses for our children. When there is a group of the population so spiritually neglected and exposed to exploitation, should we not be moved towards them, as our Saviour was? Should we not feel a sense of indignation at this state of affairs? Is it not as much an affront to God as was the challenge of Goliath to the seemingly impotent armies of Israel? Let us borrow David's phrase: 'Is there not a cause?' (1 Sam. 17:29 AV).

5.   Young children need to grow in grace. If children

become Christians then it is appropriate to teach them and encourage them in a manner suited to their capacity. The milk of the Word and the meat will both be there in the preaching. But the milk will certainly be there in the Sunday School. If it is right to notice the special needs of young men with budding gifts and to guide their reading, study and development as preachers, then it must be right, at the other end of the scale, to recognize the needs of the child. If some must be encouraged to partake of the meat, then others clearly require the pure milk.

The reality of spiritual experience for the child

The reality of child conversion

Many children of Christian parents were converted so early in their lives that they cannot remember a time when they did not believe. There are children who have been converted at the age of eight or ten, or even much earlier.

Jonathan Edwards, the great preacher and thinker of the Evangelical Awakening in America in the eighteenth century, gives accounts of very young children coming under the conviction of sin and finding peace and assurance in Christ. In *A Faithful Narrative of Surprising Conversions,* he writes, 'It has heretofore been looked on as a strange thing, when any have seemed to be savingly wrought upon and remarkably changed in their childhood. But now, I suppose, near thirty were, to appearance, savingly wrought upon, between ten and fourteen years of age; two between nine and ten, and one of about four years of age . . . The influences of God's Holy Spirit have also been very remarkable on children in some other places . . .'

Phebe Bartlett was the four-year-old of whom Edwards

spoke. She had been influenced by the conversation of her eleven-year-old brother, and in July 1735 was heard praying by her mother with earnestness and evident distress of soul, 'Pray, blessed Lord, give me salvation! I pray, beg, pardon all my sins!' When she came out of her room, she at first 'cried out aloud' and then 'continued crying, and writhing her body to and fro, like one in anguish of spirit. Her mother then asked her, whether she was afraid that God would not give her salvation. She then answered, "Yes, I am afraid I shall go to hell!"' At first she refused to be comforted, but 'at length she suddenly ceased crying, and began to smile, and presently said with a smiling countenance, "Mother, the kingdom of heaven is come to me!"' A little later, after a further time in private, she announced cheerfully to her mother, '"I can find God now!"', referring to what she had before complained of, that she could not find God. Then the child spoke again and said, "I love God!" . . . Then her elder sister, referring to her saying she could find God now, asked her where she could find God. She answered, "In heaven." "Why," said she, "Have you been in heaven?" "No," said the child. By this it seems not to have been any imagination of anything seen with bodily eyes, that she called God . . . Her mother asked her, whether she was afraid of going to hell, and if that had made her cry? She answered, "Yes, I was; but now I shan't." Her mother asked her, whether she thought that God had given her salvation: she answered, "Yes." Her mother asked her, "When?" She answered, "Today" . . . From this time there appeared a very remarkable abiding change in the child.' Edwards goes on to tell of her love of the Lord's Day, of God's house, of times of family prayer and of hearing conversation about religious matters.[1]

To take some biblical examples, the young girl who was taken captive by the Syrians and who became the slave of Naaman's wife was clearly a child of God and able to testify to the power of God (2 Kings 5:3). Josiah, the boy king of Judah, was still only a youth when he began to seek after God (2 Chron. 24:3). Timothy was already a disciple when we first read of him in Lystra (Acts 16:1), and although we do not know the time of his conversion, we do know that he had known the Scriptures from infancy (2 Tim. 3:15). We can also point to the irritation exhibited by the Lord himself when the disciples tried to keep the children from him (Mark 10:13-16). If the kingdom of God belongs to 'such as these', then it is vital to remember that the great aim of Sunday School teaching is not educative, reformative, nor moralistic, but evangelistic. It is that little children, in God's sovereign grace and good time, might be brought to saving faith in Christ. We must, as Sunday School teachers, believe in this and pray for this as the goal of all that we are doing.

Children are very often converted in large numbers in revivals
Many godly men who were used of the Lord as instruments in times of revival give accounts of children being converted in large numbers at such times. The conversion of Phebe Bartlett is only a number recorded by Jonathan Edwards during the revivals in Northampton, Massachusetts, in the eighteenth century.

Robert Murray M'Cheyne (1813–1843), whose holy life was cut short at the age of thirty, returned from a visit to the Holy Land to find a revival had occurred in his Dundee parish during his absence. He wrote to Andrew Bonar, in 1839, a letter of which the following are but a few extracts: 'I have seen many of the awakened and many of the saved:

indeed this is a pleasant place compared with what it was once . . . Some little children are evidently saved . . . One eleven years old is a singular instance of divine grace. When I asked her if she desired to be made holy, she said, "Indeed · I often wish I was awa', that I might sin nae mair." . . . A.L. of fifteen is a fine, tender-hearted believer. W.S., ten, is also a happy boy.'[2]

Asahel Nettleton, the American evangelist of the nineteenth century, has a similar account to record: 'J.B., son of E.B., aged nearly thirteen years . . . Before noon, this J. was smitten with deep conviction of sin. He continued in a distressed state about twenty-four hours, without food or sleep. His mind seemed to be overwhelmed with a sense of the dreadful nature of sin, as committed against God. Something happened to him at the end of twenty-four hours, which caused him to wipe away his tears, to wash himself, and cheerfully to partake of some food. It is now about two months since this happened. He has been, from that time to this, remarkably calm and serene in his mind. He answers questions rationally − says that he loves God and hates sin. He fails not of his daily devotions and reading the Bible, and has altogether a change of deportment. He appears to have a sense of the evil nature of sin. The duties of the Sabbath and the sanctuary appear to be his delight. It is apparent to all who know this youth, that a great change has taken place in him. From being passionate, petulant, perverse, and stubborn, he is now humble, meek, patient, forbearing, and forgiving.'[3]

While it can be argued that such conversions must have occurred under the powerful preaching of the revival, and not as the result of special classes for children, it is also true to say that our evangelical forefathers evidently had special meetings for children and that sometimes the Spirit of God fell upon the children first. The great revival of 1859 in Wales spread to some localities by means of the prayer meetings that children and young people had themselves convened. For example, 'It was not until the night of November 4th, 1859 that the full impact of the revival was felt at Dollgelley, and it came upon a children's prayer meeting in the vestry of the Calvinistic Methodist chapel.'[4] It is therefore evident that God is disposed to bless special gatherings of children.

Nettleton, too, had special meetings for the young, as the following account shows: 'To counteract the influence of these things, in the month of April, (about the time Mr. Nettleton commenced his labours in Bolton,) meetings were appointed for religious conversation with the youth, which were generally well attended, and soon became interesting. At one of these meetings eight or ten of the youth were alarmed with a sense of their sins. Their convictions deepened, until they became overwhelming; and within a few days they were brought to rejoice in hope. This spread conviction like an electric shock through the society of young people, until it was evident that the Lord had appeared in his glory to build up Zion. The volatile youth could no longer resist the influences of the Holy Spirit; but in deep solemnity were daily inquiring what they should do to be saved. Vain amusements were entirely suspended, scenes of pleasure were forsaken, and the trifles of time were lost in the awful concerns of eternity. No object could divert the anxious mind from inquiring the way to life.'[5]

The moral influence of the Sunday School in society
Although the Sunday School does not have a moral aim, it is undeniable that it has a moral influence. Even if children in the Sunday School do not come to faith in Christ, and

Spiritual experience and the child

eventually leave unconverted, yet the attitudes and ideals learnt in Sunday School may remain with them to the end of their lives. Many of today's older generation, although not Christians, still remember their time in Sunday School and show some affection for the things learnt there. This is not to defend the frail morality of a second-hand religion, but simply to emphasize that the Sunday School teacher may yet act as 'salt and light' in the community, even if the children under his or her care are never converted. Naturally we should not be happy to see our children merely made outwardly moral, and we must at all costs avoid the unfortunate tendency in some Sunday Schools to aim at nothing more than that. Yet, short of the children's conversion, which must always be our aim, it cannot be bad for society if their thinking and moral standards are influenced by biblical truths which they learned in Sunday School.

1. For the full account, see Jonathan Edwards, *Complete Works*, vol. 1, pp. 361—363, Banner of Truth Trust.
2. A. Bonar, *Memoirs & Remains of R.M. M'Cheyne*, Banner of Truth Trust, p. 118.
3. B. Tyler and A. Bonar, *The Life and Labours of Asahel Nettleton*, Banner of Truth Trust, p. 77.
4. E. Evans, *When He is Come*, EPW, p. 105.
5. *Life & Labours of Asahel Nettleton*, p. 107.

3.
The Sunday School teacher's pedigree

There may be those who would point a finger at the Sunday School teacher and demand that he identify himself in biblical terms. I hope that what we have seen from the Scriptures so far will give every teacher an adequate answer to that. It should strengthen the hand of every teacher to know that he or she is not a kind of spiritual mongrel, but comes from a good pedigree of Christian men and women whose principles were biblical and whose hearts were warm and sincere in their desire to spread the gospel among children.

The practice of Sunday School teaching is often criticized because it was not in vogue in a period when the spiritual life of our country was very full and rich, namely the Puritan period in the sixteenth century. It is argued that, at this time of high spirituality and gospel blessing, no conces-sions were made for children and that the only ministry they received was from the pulpit. It simply is not true that the Puritans made no special attempts to instruct their children. 'If the quip is true that variety is the spice of life, the Puritan view of children in the church certainly provides rich sustenance.' This is the view of R. Philip Roberts in his paper, 'The Puritan View of Children in the Church'.[1] There were not only a variety of views among the Puritans about the place of children in the church but a variety of approaches in catering for them. The widespread practice of catechizing by the minister himself is a testimony to this. 'Edward Morgan in his book *The Puritan Family* also has ably demonstrated the thoroughness of the New England Puritans in the religious instruction of their offspring. Several churches in the seventeenth century, he noted, "sometimes had assemblies of children resembling Sunday Schools, for the purpose of catechizing" as well as having "chosen select men" of every town "to go occasionally from house to house and test the children's knowledge of their catechisms". This concern and interest in education was universal among Puritans of virtually all groups and factions on both sides of the Atlantic.'[2]

In fact, the Puritans were noted for their concern for the religious education of the young. The fact that for some of them this virtually obliterated the need for the regeneration of their children must not be overlooked, but certainly underlines the point. It was especially the Baptists and John Bunyan in particular who, far from abandoning the attempt to instruct children, specifically insisted that the teaching should be evangelical in character and aimed at bringing the children to an acknowledgement of their sin and their need of Christ: 'Ah! Poor sweet babes, the Lord open their eyes, and make them holy Christians. Saith David, "Come ye children, hearken unto me; I will teach you the fear of the Lord" (Ps. 34:11). He doth not say, "I will muzzle you up in a form of prayer"; but "I will teach you the fear of the Lord"; which is, to see their sad states by nature, and to be instructed in the truth of the gospel, which doth through the Spirit beget prayer in everyone that in truth learns it. And the more you learn them this, the more will their hearts run out to God in prayer. God never did account Paul a praying man, until he was a convinced and converted man; no more will be it with any else.'[3] R. Philip Roberts adds the following comment: 'In this instruction there is no presumption that children are in any way holy. The emphasis is less didactic, it stresses more strongly the immediate work of the Spirit; it is aimed at the heart as well as the head and the conversion of children is its desire. Where doctrines are taught to children it must be done to persuade them to embrace the gospel. In no case should it be presumed that believers' children hold the truth in sincerity.'

The history of the Sunday School as we know it goes back to Robert Raikes in 1780. The *Gloucester Journal* reports, 'The children were to come soon after ten in the morning and stay till twelve. They were then to go home and stay till one: after reading the lesson they were to be conducted to church. After church they were to be employed in repeating the catechism till half past five and then to be dismissed with an injunction to go home without making a noise and by no means to play in the street.' Raikes employed four women to do this at the cost of one shilling a day.[4] While Robert Raikes was not the outstanding evangelical that many have represented him to be, and though his work may have been more reformative in nature than evangelical, yet it was a sincere response to the appalling social conditions that prevailed 200 years ago. 'It may well be that the work of Robert Raikes himself should be put to a large extent into the category of "common grace" or "restraining grace" rather than that of "special grace".'[5] Were we to have opposed it on the grounds that it was not sufficiently evangelical we would have found ourselves in the company of such non-evangelicals as the High Church Bishop of Rochester and out of sympathy with such servants of God as John and Charles Wesley and John Newton.

The question is raised, 'Should we not respond to the prevailing appalling spiritual condition of the children of our generation?' Declared Wesley, 'Unless we take care of the rising generation the present revival of religion will only last the age of a man.' And to his class leaders he gave the following directive: 'Spend one hour a week with the children, whether you like it or not!' Henry Martyn, the missionary, confessed in 1884, 'Extremely diligent in the humble but most enjoyable task of catechizing the children.'

Charles Haddon Spurgeon rejoiced to recollect that his first efforts were among the children in the Sunday School and expressed his approval of that work in these terms: 'I love to see persons of some standing in society take an interest in Sabbath Schools. One great fault in many of our churches is that the children are left for the young people to take care of; the older members, who have more wisdom, taking but very little notice of them; and very often, the wealthier members of the church stand aside as if the teaching of the poor were not (as indeed it is) the special business of the rich. I hope for the day when the mighty men of Israel shall be found helping in this great warfare against the enemy. In the United States, we have heard of presidents, judges, members of Congress, and persons in the highest positions, not condescending — for I scorn to use such a term — but honouring themselves by teaching little children in Sabbath Schools. He who teaches a class in a Sabbath School has earned a good degree. I had rather receive the title of S.S.T. than M.A., B.A., or any other honour that ever was conferred by men.'

We must therefore be convinced of the spirituality of this work, its biblical basis and our own calling to it. How shall we become so convinced? By meditating upon the spiritual condition of the children and remembering that they are born in sin and, until they are born again, are bound for hell, whether sprinkled with water or not, dedicated or not! The general tenor of biblical teaching should commend the practice to us. The tenderness of the Lord Jesus Christ should commend it, as well as the example of the saints through the ages. Ezra the priest brought the Word of God to the whole assembly of men, women and children. The law was addressed to 'all who could understand' (Neh. 8). Let us make it our ambition to bring the Word of God to all who can hear it with understanding and also to do so in a manner corresponding to their level of understanding.

Let us give Jonathan Edwards the last word: 'What has more especially given offence to many, and raised a loud cry against some preachers, as though their conduct were intolerable, is their frightening poor innocent children with talk of hell-fire, and eternal damnation. But if those who complain so loudly of this, really believe what is the general profession of the country, viz. that all are by nature children of wrath and heirs of hell — and that everyone that has not been born again, whether he be young or old, is exposed every moment to eternal destruction . . . Innocent as children seem to us, yet, if they are out of Christ, they are not so in the sight of God; but are in a most miserable condition, as well as grown persons . . . Why should we conceal the truth from them? Will those children who have been dealt tenderly with in this respect, and lived and died insensible of their misery till they come to feel it in hell, ever thank parents and others for their tenderness, in not letting them know their danger?'[6]

1. *Westminster Conference Papers 1980.*
2. As above.
3. J. Bunyan, 'On Praying in the Spirit', *Complete Works*, vol. 1, p. 635.
4. A brief but good account of the work of Robert Raikes can be read in the 1980 Westminster Conference Report.
5. John Carrick, 'Robert Raikes and the Origin of Sunday Schools', *Westminster Conference Papers*, 1980, p. 84.
6. J. Edwards, *Complete Works*, vol. 1, pp. 361–363.

Part II

Sunday School: the practical outworking

4.
Who should teach?—The teacher's qualifications

In many Sunday Schools, while great care is taken concerning the lesson materials, equipment and an up-to-date approach to the work, the most important factor, namely the qualifications of the teacher, is sadly neglected. The key to fruitful Sunday School teaching is the teacher. Methods and materials, however excellent, will fail unless the teachers are 'full of faith and of the Holy Spirit' (Acts 6:5). In many churches teaching is left to the young, inexperienced Christians, who are started off in their teaching career with the nursery class because these children are considered to be the most manageable. The Sunday School does offer an avenue for young Christians to begin to exercise their gifts, but too often the desire to get a young person working outweighs more important criteria. The teaching of the children must not be placed second in importance to the desire to engage enthusiastic teenagers in the work. Often the difficulty of finding a suitable teacher is solved too conveniently by this method, to the spiritual detriment of both the little children and the young people concerned.

Spurgeon said, 'One great fault in many of our churches is that the children are left for the young people to take care of; the older members, who have more wisdom, taking but very little notice of them . . .' He was clearly not in favour of leaving the work of the Sunday School to the young people. On the other hand, he did not debar the young and enthusiastic servant of the Lord from taking up the work, for, 'There is no time for work like the first hours of the day; and there is no time for serving the Lord like the very earliest days of youth. I recollect the joy I had in the little service I was able to render to God when first I knew him.' We must conclude therefore that age alone neither qualifies nor disqualifies for the work. The following paragraphs summarize the basic qualifications for taking up the work of a Sunday School teacher.

1. The teacher must be saved

The Sunday School teacher must not only be a believer, but he must be one who is assured of his salvation and has a clear grasp of the way of salvation. No one can fruitfully teach the gospel, which is 'the power of God for salvation', unless he has known the reality of it in his own life. Spurgeon says of the time when he was engaged in the work of a Sunday School, 'When I began to teach — I was very young in grace then — I said to the class of boys whom I was teaching, Jesus Christ saved all those who believed in him. One of them at once asked me the question: "Teacher, do *you* believe in him?" I replied, "Yes, I hope I do." Then he enquired again, "But are you not sure?" I had to think carefully what answer I should give. The lad was not content with my repeating, "I hope so." He would have it, "If you have believed in Christ, you *are* saved." And I felt at that time that I could not teach effectually until I could say positively, "I know that it is so. I must be able to speak of what I have heard, and seen, and tasted, and handled of the

good Word of life." The boy was right; there can be no true
testimony except that which springs from assured conviction
of our own safety and joy in the Lord.'[1] Thus the teacher is
a person of humility, faith and obedience towards God.

2. The teacher must be separated

Our salvation and the call to service demand that everything
that is out of character with the holiness of God must be
renounced and avoided (Rom. 12:1, 2). The best illustration
of every lesson given in Sunday School should be the
teacher's own life. To this end, the teacher must seek after
a holy life and a close walk with God. There must be a
seriousness about him that will impress upon the child the
importance of Christian things (Luke 6:39, 40). The prayer-
less Christian cannot expect to encourage his class to
become prayerful or to take any notice of what he teaches
about prayer. The joyless Christian cannot impart a sense of
the reality of spiritual joy to his class members.

There is also to be a separation to the work (Rom. 1:1).
A prospective Sunday School teacher should be prepared to
make the commitments listed below or else not take up the
work. In addition to his other commitments as a church
member, every teacher should endeavour to

a. Spend an equivalent of one evening per week in
preparation and, where necessary, in visitation.

b. Arrive at the class at least fifteen minutes before
school starts, so as to be ready for the children, and
also to be available to talk to the parents. He must be
prepared to remain behind to tidy up and must not
try to do this during the end of his lesson.

c. Plan occasional extra activities for the children, such

as outings, teas, parties, etc.
d. Pray for each member of his class regularly.
e. Attend all the meetings arranged for preparation and teachers' discussions about the work of the Sunday School.

Writing on 'First things First in Teaching', Peter Jeffery says, 'Your first duty is to live close to God, to have a healthy, vibrant spiritual life. Robert Murray M'Cheyne rightly said, "It is not so much great talents that God blesses, as great likeness to Christ." The teacher who is close to his Saviour will teach the Scriptures with an inevitable zeal and earnestness and devotion that the Holy Spirit will take delight in.'[2]

Four important spiritual questions must therefore be faced regularly by every teacher if he desires to be effective. They are

a. Does my life glorify God?
b. Are my life and my message Christ-centred?
c. Am I committed wholly to the spiritual welfare of the children I teach?
d. Does the Holy Spirit empower my teaching? If you ask him to do this, he will. It is a thrilling experience when the teacher feels that the Holy Spirit has shown him the lesson in the text and brought it home to his heart.

3. The teacher must be sent

Good Sunday School teachers are not just people filling in their time or enjoying doing a bit of work for the church. In the first place, they must feel called and commissioned by the Lord Jesus Christ himself. Without this sense of calling the whole work may prove to be too demanding (Matt. 28:19, 20).

Secondly, because this work calls for the exercise of talents and gifts, there must also be a corresponding recognition and sending of the teachers on the part of the local church. Church members, elders and pastors must be on the look-out for those who display gifts in dealing with their own children, coupled with a basic grasp of gospel truth. Such people must be sent, or set apart, by the church for the work. None must be allowed to proceed apart from this recognition (read 2 Sam. 18:19-33). If you are not sent in this way it usually means that Christians with a degree of spirituality and good judgement do not feel that you have a gift to exercise or a message to deliver. The practice of asking for volunteers for this work is to be discouraged. Only those with some aptitude and ability should be asked to teach.

Clearly those who are sent are to be the representatives and agents of the whole church. No Sunday School must be allowed to become a little kingdom within the church, and no Sunday School teacher must seek to operate as if he were a law unto himself. Sunday School teaching is a part of the work and service of the whole church and it must be seen as an extension of the church's work. Every teacher must therefore regard himself as responsible and answerable to the church officers and church meeting and, ultimately, to God. Consequently all Sunday School teachers should be

a. Full members of the local church.
b. Regular at all the church services, especially the prayer meeting and Bible study. Attendance at the former will ensure that the needs of the Sunday School are regularly brought before the members in the prayer meeting, and attendance at the latter will ensure that the teacher, who is giving out so much, will regularly be taking in spiritual instruction and

food. This is vital, since the Sunday School teacher is handling the Word of God and instructing young lives in Christian faith and doctrine. It is essential that the teacher should himself be taught and grounded in the truth. Correct doctrine is as important in the Sunday School as anywhere else.

c. Ready to recognize the authority and discipline of the local church and their own responsibilities within it.

The teacher's work is a vital and a sacred one.

4. The teacher must be studious

The teacher must know thoroughly what is being taught. Moreover he must have grasped it before he teaches it. Frequently teachers have testified to the fact that they only really came to understand a doctrine when they grappled with it in order to be able to teach it simply to the children. Professional men spend years in study. It would not do if the doctor had to refer to his textbook to find out what to do when the patient was in the throes of a heart attack! It is just as disastrous when a teacher endeavours to communicate a lesson or a truth which is only partially known and ill-digested. Any teacher who has to consult his lesson manual in the midst of a lesson must regard that lesson as a failure.

The following are essentials for a studious teacher:

a. Implicit confidence in the Word of God. It is the teacher's duty always to explain it, but never to explain it away. The miraculous must be left starkly supernatural.

b. Daily reading of, and meditation on the Bible. The teacher must be familiar with the appropriate passage of the Bible and adept at applying it. That is to say, the teacher must be sure that his use of Scripture is apt, that he has gone to the most appropriate story or text, and is not 'bending' Scripture to fit his lesson.

c. A grasp of related subjects, such as the background to the Bible, its geography, its history and its customs.

d. A sound knowledge of the great doctrines of the Christian faith. He must understand the doctrinal terminology which he may find in his teacher's manual, so that he will be able to simplify it for the children.

e. Adequate study of the lesson material, going far beyond what will be required in the lesson to be given to the children. The teacher must give them the cream! This means a severe discipline and a commitment to begin study early in the week (some suggest that the first reading of the lesson material ought to occupy the Sunday evening of the week before), so that the lesson can develop and 'gel' in the mind during the course of the week. Too often the teacher — and the preacher also — comes away from his teaching regretting a hasty preparation and realizing too late the way in which that particular truth ought to have been presented.

f. Ability to deliver well-prepared lessons that are the teacher's own. He must use the lesson-help booklet to prepare lessons of his own in such a way that he not only does not need the lesson manual in the class, but that, even if he took it with him, it would be inadequate.

All of this takes time, prayer and thought. It has been

said that there is no expedient to which a man will not stoop to avoid the painful necessity of thinking! Teachers must be thinkers. There is no substitute for good solid thought.

5. The teacher must be sensible

A primary school teacher was once asked what he taught. He replied, 'Children!' The trouble with too many teachers is that they teach 'geography' or 'history' quite well, but unfortunately never relate the subject to the children. A sensible teacher will adjust his approach to the needs of the child. There are two approaches to Sunday School teaching. One is to be 'Bible-centred' and the other is to be 'child-centred'. In the latter approach the Bible is reduced to a mere resource from which to draw materials applicable to a child's problems or situation. The Bible becomes a kind of spiritual *Aesop's Fables,* a collection of moralistic stories to help one through life. Now there is all the difference in the world between being 'child-centred' and endeavouring to apply the truths of the Bible to the children in the class. To begin with Scripture and to wrestle with the problem of making it simple for the child is much more difficult and requires much more thought and skill than the child-centred approach. It has been said, 'The child's mind is a citadel that can be taken neither by stealth nor by storm; but there is a natural way of approach and a gate of easy entry always open to him who knows how to find it.' An unscrupulous teacher will soon find out that children can neither be duped nor forced into beliefs which they do not have, and should remember that a man whose opinion is changed against his will is of the same opinion still.

Later in our studies we shall consider some fundamental techniques of speaking to the child and of gaining and keeping his attention. The teacher is to be sensible, that is, he is to be sensitive to the needs of the child and sensible in his own approach to the child. Many pitfalls can be avoided by sheer common sense.

It is necessary to get to know the children individually, their home backgrounds, capabilities and interests. The aim is to be sensitive to the children so that the biblical truth we bring them in each lesson will be presented to them in a way which is suitable to their background, level of understanding and experience.

For further study and reflection
1. Read Romans 12.
2. Write down what impressed you most about a teacher (Sunday School or otherwise) who has helped you in the past. In what way did you learn certain truths which are now precious to you?
3. Why do you want to teach in Sunday School and what do you think a call to be a teacher is?
4. Discuss some of these issues in your Sunday School teachers' meetings.

1. C.H. Spurgeon. *The Early Years*, Banner of Truth Trust, p. 157.
2. P. Jeffery. 'First Things First in Teaching', *Go Teach – Teachers' Manual for Young Teenagers*.

5.
Why teach?—The teacher's aim

What is the task of the Sunday School teacher? There may
be many, but the chief one is surely to convey to the
children the body of truth contained in the Bible in a
manner appropriate to their age and intelligence. Throughout the Bible we find the charge to commit to our children
the truths of Scripture. This duty is repeated throughout
the Old Testament (Gen. 18:19; Exod. 10:2; 12:26, 27;
13:14-16; Deut. 4:9, 10; 6:4-9; Isa. 8:19, 20). Timothy had
benefited from such instruction (2 Tim. 1:5; 3:15).

We have already noticed that Sunday School teaching is
to be seen as supplementary to the responsibilities of the
parent. There is evidence of such supplementary teaching in
the Old Testament. 'Although at first the education of
children was viewed as the sole task and responsibility of
the parents, at a later period priests and Levites, prophets
and special tutors, "wise men", scribes and rabbis all
contributed their share in raising the cultural level of the
youth of the nation.'[1]

How then can we summarize the specific aims of the
Sunday School teacher?

1. Teaching the whole counsel of God

The teacher must see it as his duty to commit to the young the contents and the message of the Bible. It is the revelation of God that is to be the subject matter of our teaching. We must never allow the lesson to slide into a nice little moralizing story, a kind of biblical *Aesop's Fable* with a moral tag line. On the contrary, the teacher is to teach the Bible and endeavour to cover all its main stories and themes in the course of a given syllabus. He must

a. Evangelize

This does not mean to say that we are looking to elicit the immediate response of saving faith all the time. Our view must be more long-term than that. The truth of the Bible is given to us in order that sinners might be convicted of their sin and brought to Christ. We must never lose sight of that aim (Matt. 19:13, 14).

b. Instruct

It is part of the task to instruct the children and to put into their minds the instructions of the Lord. Children need to be taught what is right and what is wrong in the sight of God. They need to learn what God requires of them. In the days in which we live no one else is going to tell them this. The Sunday School teacher will no doubt be told by modern educators that it is wrong to impose standards on the young and that he must rather endeavour to bring out that which is innate in the child and help him to develop his own morality, one which works for him, and thus maintain the integrity of the child's individuality. Such an approach totally ignores the doctrine of the Fall and the depravity of human nature. To ask children vague questions, such as

'Why do you do such things?' (1 Sam. 2:23), and to expect that they can supply their own answer and reason out their own standards of right and wrong, is misguided and hopeless humanist idealism. A Sunday School teacher whose lessons aim at this goal will be a miserable failure. 'God demands that when questions are asked, definite answers should be given!'[2] (Exod. 13:8; Deut. 6:20-25). Children are to be taught God's statutes. The practice of catechizing, that is, asking a question and teaching a biblical answer supported by a Scripture, is a neglected but most useful practice.

c. Relate

The teacher must endeavour to understand the implications of what is being taught and to relate that particular lesson to the child's overall responsibility to serve God. If God requires of man the recognition of his lordship, this has implications in every department of life. The particular lesson therefore is capable of being related to (a) the varied situations in which the child finds himself — at home, at school, or among his friends, and (b) the general requirements of prayer, praise and obedience which we all owe to God. The place of the child in worship and the relationship of the Sunday School to the life of the local church will also have to be considered.

The pursuits of the Sunday School must be seen to be an integrated part of the service and ministry of the local church as a whole. Children must be made to feel that they belong in the worship services of the church and not that 'church' is for grown-ups and 'Sunday School' for them. So often in the past a chasm has been created between the children and the life of the church, with disastrous results. Either the children cease to attend when they have outgrown Sunday School or, in a desperate attempt to keep them, the mistake is made of building up a parallel structure in which young people, and young adults well into their twenties, are catered for — but never attend church.

The worship of God, as our overall duty, must, then, be shown to the children as something that we all do together. Let the lambs run with the flock. In this way a bridge will be made for them between Sunday School and church, and church attendance and worship will be shown to be necessary accompaniments to Sunday School and not an unwelcome alternative. Children will also be introduced to preaching in this way. Teachers ought to be prepared to have the children in their class sit with them during the service if the parents do not attend church. Let teacher and child worship together and let example go hand in hand with precept.

However, none of these practical matters, by which we try to relate what is taught in Sunday School to life in general and to the life of the local church in particular, must be allowed to blind the teacher, or the parent for that matter, to a very real danger. No child, whether of Christian parents or otherwise, will become a true worshipper of God without being born again. No matter how well our teaching is related to the life of the church, nor how integrated the Sunday School is with the worship of the church, young people are not made Christians by integration nor by smooth transition from one age group to another. Many foolish errors have been made at this point — only for disillusion to set in for the teacher, the church and, more important, for the child himself on arriving at adulthood. The emptiness of church attendance without a real and living faith in Christ has led many to leave and to dismiss the whole thing as adolescent infatuation.

2. Teaching the children

All that we have said so far means that our teaching has to be Bible-centred, but we must also remember that we are teaching children. The watchword of our teaching thus becomes 'Bible-centred and child-orientated'.

Here again we must beware of the many voices of modern secular education, which will warn us against too much emphasis on learning by heart, on the one hand, and against trying to teach abstract concepts far beyond the limits of young children, on the other. Obviously it is right to take care not to talk over the child's head. Aim at simplicity. However, the opposite danger is just as real. Do not be babyish. Do not be silly and do not talk down in a condescending kind of way. A great deal of imagination will be needed to discover what interests children of a given age, so that suitable illustrations can be used and their interest kept. Remember (a) the spiritual state of the child; (b) the need to interest him; (c) the work of the Holy Spirit. Not even adults in their natural state can receive the Word of God, but under the Spirit's influence children as well as adults are able to grasp spiritual concepts and truths.

Let us hold on to two facts which have been proved over many years of Sunday School teaching.

1.   There is great value in memorizing lessons and especially Scripture, even when the meaning is not fully comprehended at the time. Many children have learnt by rote passages of the Bible, or the questions, answers and proof texts of a catechism, without really understanding them. The truths learned have remained dormant for years. Unconsciously such knowledge has moulded their habits and attitudes, but, even more importantly, it has represented a golden store which has been of tremendous benefit in later years,

after they have been born again. Memorization is not the be-all and end-all of teaching, but it should have its place. If we cannot hide God's Word in a child's heart, at least we can attempt to hide it in his memory. To do this is like laying the paper and sticks for a coal fire and then placing on the dark coals. The fuel is ready and when it is eventually ignited what a blaze there will be! Men of previous generations were able to use Scriptures and preach sermons of great maturity within weeks or months of their conversion. How did they acquire such a facility? The answer is that they had the Scriptures already in store!

Children are not often taught to memorize things these days. This is a great deficiency in modern education and will mean that we are engaged in a battle to persuade the children and to train them in the art of memorization, but we must do it! (Isa. 28:9, 10.)

2.   Never underestimate what a child can understand of spiritual truth. This is the great answer to those who object to teaching young children spiritual truths and also to those who object to keeping children in the services during the preaching. The preaching may not be aimed precisely at them, but they do receive far more than we think. If spiritual truths are spiritually discerned, then the Spirit of God can reveal spiritual truths even to young children (1 Cor. 1:18-20, 27-29; 2:12). Indeed childlike simplicity of mind may be an advantage in the receiving of basic truths. 'Unless you . . . become like little children, you will never enter the kingdom of heaven' (Matt. 18:3). Read once more the story of four-year-old Phebe Bartlett related in chapter 2.

Two major questions remain to be considered.

1. Are we to teach doctrine or the Bible?

The answer is 'Both!', because the Bible is full of doctrine, or teaching. Then the question becomes 'Should we teach a doctrinal system, or simply teach the Bible stories and passages in a non-systematic, disconnected way?' The answer to this question is 'Neither!' The teacher will need to know a system of doctrine as the framework for his teaching of the Bible so that, as the Bible is taught, truths can be identified, taught clearly and simply and, where appropriate, related to other truths.

The importance of the teacher's grasp of basic doctrine now emerges. He has to be able to see the doctrine in the passage and draw it out simply and plainly. (A later section will discuss the helps vital to enable the teacher to do this.) The teacher must be on the look-out for the 'big' spiritual truths.

The teacher is

a. To be aware of the church's doctrinal basis. These doctrines are a good summary of those that need to be known and taught.

b. To grasp the significance of the major doctrines and to see their application to life. He must be able to show their relevance to the children.

c. To make sure he has a full grasp of those doctrines directly bearing on salvation, so that he can see the connections between one truth and another and identify the various steps in the process of salvation.

d. To apply the standards and demands of God's Word and to identify the vital principles which govern a life lived in the fear of God.

Please do not give up at this point! We must all strive to be relevant and to apply the great truths of Scripture to those who listen to us, be they adults or children. To succeed in the role of teachers we must all continue to be learners. We must constantly be reading and filling our minds and hearts with Christian truth, so that we may be able to teach it to others. We need to re-emphasize the needs of the teacher's own heart. He must be regularly under the ministry of his own church, especially at the Bible studies and the teaching sermons. Those churches that run a Sunday School concurrently with the morning service are thus depriving the teachers, those who most need to be taking in, from receiving the very sustenance which would enrich their own teaching ministry.

2. How are we to make biblical truths relevant to the children?

We shall consider some practical ways later, but for the moment let us consider four principles.

1.   There has to be a point of contact. When the teacher has isolated and identified the truth to be imparted, he has to settle on some point of application. This application does not always have to come at the end. It can come at the beginning of his lesson, or at the end, or both. Sometimes it is most helpful to start with it, so that the relevance of what follows is already evident to the children. Although the lesson may begin with the application, the preparation does not! This would be to lapse into 'child-centred' or 'situation-centred' teaching, which slips easily into a moralizing approach, with texts and Bible stories simply tagged on to a moral lesson. The point of contact is not to be the controlling factor. It is simply the result of the teacher's asking himself how he can apply the teaching of that

51

particular passage to the children in front of him. The need is to build a bridge from the Bible to the child, over which the truth may be conveyed.

2.   The best way of fixing spiritual truths in the minds of children is by telling them a story. 'If I was ever a little dull, my scholars began to make wheels of themselves, twisting round on the forms on which they sat. That was a very plain intimation to me that I must give them an illustration or an anecdote, and I learned to tell stories partly by being obliged to tell them. One boy, who I had in the class, used to say to me, "This is very dull, teacher; can't you pitch us a yarn?" Of course, he was a naughty boy, and it might be supposed that he went to the bad when he grew up, though I am not at all sure that he did, but I used to try and pitch him the yarn that he wanted, in order to get his attention again.'[3]

If the Bible passage is itself a story, use it faithfully but imaginatively. By the skilful use of Bible stories vital doctrines can be taught, not merely painlessly, but enjoyably and profitably. Keep the following rules:

   a. Never be content merely to tell a story.
   b. Be imaginative and lively, but always draw out plainly the simple teaching involved.
   c. Concentrate on the big, simple truths. Teach them again and again, in different lessons and in different ways.
   d. Beware of 'hobby horses', that is, of reading into the story things that are not there. This is especially a danger when dealing with parables. We shall consider this problem further in a later chapter.

3.   Teach what has gripped your own heart. It was Bunyan who testified, 'I preached what I smartingly did feel.' Now all teachers should have a longing to bring the children to

see their need of Christ. However, more specifically, the Sunday School teacher must pray his lesson into his own heart and experience until he is gripped by that particular truth. Never, never simply repeat a lesson out of a book. If it has not gripped the teacher, it will not grip the child; if the teacher is not enthusiastic about it, the child is sure to be bored. The teacher should never be in a strait-jacket with respect to his Sunday School booklet. It is little wonder that children tire of Sunday School at an early age if they have simply been fed a diet of second-hand ideas from a booklet — yesterday's manna, stale and mouldy. The Sunday School teacher must make use of every aid and all study notes to prepare *his own lesson,* but he must take to the children what God has given him with the conviction that 'This is God's lesson for this class this Sunday'.

1. Hendriksen — *Commentary on 1 and 2 Timothy*, Banner of Truth Trust, p. 298.
2. As above.
3. C.H. Spurgeon: *The Early Years*, Banner of Truth Trust, p. 158.

6.
What is teaching?—The teacher's work

It is not accidental that school teaching is described as 'work'. Even Paul testifies to the laborious nature of the calling to teach (Col. 1:28, 29). Listen also to the testimony of the Puritan, John Flavel, in describing the duties of the pastoral ministry: 'The labours of the ministry will exhaust the very marrow from your bones . . . And, indeed, it is not so much the expense of our labours, as the loss of them, that kills us. It is not with us, as with other labourers: they find their work as they leave it; so do not we. Sin and Satan unravel almost all we do, the impressions we make on our people's souls in one sermon vanish before the next.'[1]

Anyone who has spent any length of time as a Sunday School teacher will know something of the weekly labours needed to maintain the interest of the children. Along with William Carey, every teacher needs 'grace to plod'!

The New Testament has a great deal to say about teaching. Teaching formed the major part of Christ's ministry. The Gospels contain forty-five references to his teaching and he was called 'Teacher' or some similar title, about 100 times. This is significant in view of the many other ways he might have chosen in which to fulfil his mission. A study of Christ's teaching is very revealing and instructive and provides an insight into the vastness of the work.

As we saw in chapter 1, a great deal of informal teaching went on within the local church besides the more formal ministry of the pastor and teacher. This informal activity is an outworking of the priesthood of all believers. The Sunday School teacher is himself subject to the teaching ministry of his church and his work is supplementary to that of the parent. Moreover, to the children of non-Christian homes he is the only teacher of Christianity they are likely to have.

The New Testament pattern, and especially the teaching ministry of the Lord, makes it clear that 'teaching' is not simply 'lecturing', nor passing on information and facts. It is much wider and deeper and includes the following elements.

1. Guiding

Through the study of the Bible, the teacher aims to guide and help the young to face the problems of conduct and attitude which they are likely to meet. This is achieved by applying Bible principles. This is what the Lord was doing constantly with his hearers. In any given situation he was not only dealing with the needs of others or challenging the Pharisees, but guiding his disciples and moulding their thinking and attitudes (Matt. 12:46-50; Mark 8:14-21; John 12:27-33). The Gospels are simply full of such examples.

2. Sharing

Teaching depends almost one hundred per cent on the

formation of a relationship of mutual trust and love and a ready acceptance on both sides of the twin roles of teacher and taught. With a little reflection this becomes almost too obvious to need saying, and yet it is so often overlooked. Teachers tend to think they have a right to teach and the student a duty to learn. No, No! Teaching is a privilege which is accorded to the teacher by the taught. The role of teacher is, then, something accorded by the pupil and that role will not be accorded unless there is a respect for the person. This respect has to be won by genuinely giving oneself to the pupil, as the result of a real and deep love. So many teachers, both spiritual and secular, have deluded themselves that an official status accorded to them is all that they need in order to demand the submission of their pupils. No real teaching can exist in those circumstances. The teacher–pupil relationship is a shared one of giving and receiving, and not simply the passing on of information. The teacher must give himself to the pupil. Only then can the teaching process begin.

How foolish is the preacher or teacher who thinks only of himself and his gift, imagined or real, and concludes that on that account alone people are sure to listen to him, and that simply because he is exercising his gift they are bound to say, 'Amen' to whatever he might chance to say! That is folly. The only true motive for teaching is a heartfelt desire to be the servant of the taught, and the giving of oneself utterly for the good of the students. This is nowhere more beautifully set forth than in the relationship between Christ and his disciples. Why did they follow him, accept his 'discipline' and learn of him? It was because he gave himself unreservedly to them. They desired him to be their teacher (John 1:35-39; Mark 3:13-18; John 13:1).

3. Discovering

Discovering truth for oneself is real learning. An old Chinese proverb goes something like this: 'I hear and I forget, I see and I remember, I do and I understand.' This principle has been exploited well in the use of mechanical blocks and other apparatus in the teaching of maths, for example, in primary school. Children actually handling the materials learn the values and understand their numerical relationships. Now this proverb must not be pressed absolutely. 'Faith comes by hearing'! I use it simply to underline the need for the pupil to enter in, to be involved in some measure, in order truly to learn. Helping a child to discover truth for himself is real teaching. This does not mean leaving him to flounder with questions to which he must find his own answers, but rather to guide and to help him to discover the answers of the Word of God to the needs and the questions of his own life. We want children to see the truth, not because the teacher says so, but because the Bible says so (Mark 10:17-30; 14:27-31) and because it is relevant to them.

4. Building

Nothing must be assumed in teaching the Bible. We have to start at the beginning with the basic truths and build up, little by little, a body of biblical knowledge (Isa. 28:9, 10). This can be viewed in two ways. Firstly, we can consider it as beginning with the simple truths about God and man, then, during the course of a child's progress through the Sunday School syllabus and in the young people's group, going on to the understanding of the broad and basic doctrines of the Christian faith. The simple basic concepts must be grasped before we build other doctrines upon them (John 16:12). Secondly, this building process can be viewed in a more spiritual way. As the Bible is taught, Christ himself must be shown to be the centre and theme of it all. Everything must be founded upon Christ (Eph. 2:20-22).

5. Correcting

When children come to Sunday School, not only must we not assume any pre-existing knowledge, but we must also be prepared for those who come with strange and erroneous notions. Some of these ideas will be based on the general ignorance that is abroad about the things of God, some on humanistic teaching received in day school and others, more deeply rooted, will be little better than superstitions derived from life in a family who may have had no direct contact with biblical teaching for generations. Sometimes the teacher will have to fill out rather hollow, bare concepts and at other times correct totally wrong ideas which the children may have. An example of the filling out can be found in Acts 17:22, 23. Teachers must be alert for these opportunities and use the vague knowledge the child offers as an opening into which fuller teaching may be grafted. The direct correcting of inherited and wrong ideas must be handled more delicately, but no less definitely (1 Tim 1:3; Matt. 15:15-20).

6. Understanding

All that has already been said serves to emphasize the need

for the teacher to get to know his children and to understand them as individuals. Few children ever learn anything well unless they need it and realize this need. How are we to discover their needs? Here are some suggestions:

a. Get to know the children individually and intimately. Know the names of all the class. The teacher can then think intelligently about them as individuals and pray for them in the same way. This means that the teacher must make contact with them outside the Sunday School. Their homes should be visited and, if possible, the teacher's home should be open to the children. Have them to tea or to a party.

b. Gain the confidence of the children, so that they will reveal their needs. It is far better for the children to do this than for the teacher to have to discover the needs by undue searching and probing. In this way the teacher will be able to gauge his own relationship with the children.

c. Learn the 'age characteristics' of your class. You should aim at becoming a specialist in the understanding of your particular age group. Consider well the age group of your children: are they beginners, primary or junior? Find out their current interests and activities.

d. Keep a record. This should be a confidential account of your understanding of each child's needs. Weekly contacts will provide fresh data for this record and it will be useful to refer to during lesson preparation.

e. Pray for wisdom. God has promised this to those who ask in faith (James 1:5). It would be utterly foolish to become wise in your own eyes and consider yourself entirely able to discern all the needs of others. This is an ability that God alone possesses, but he has promised to help us.

Conclusion

It can be seen that teaching is much more than relating a weekly lesson in a mechanical way. The question now naturally occurs: 'How can we make pupils conscious of their needs?' The answer to this lies in the power of the Holy Spirit, for he alone can convince of sin, righteousness and judgement. We therefore need to seek his endowment for our work and his enlightenment of those we teach. This does not cancel out our responsibility, for, as teachers, we need to conduct our classes in a way that is honouring to God. How can we ask the Holy Spirit to bless work of which we ourselves may be ashamed? This means having a clearly defined aim and objective to begin with, as well as satisfactory lesson content and procedure. The attaining of our objectives will be covered in later lessons, but let us be perfectly clear about our real goal, which is to lead children to receive and confess the Lord Jesus Christ and to help them to fulfil God's will in their lives. This also means leading them into an understanding of the ways and purposes of God.

For further study:

1. Read Mark's Gospel and consider Christ's method of teaching.
2. Are aims essential to teaching? Why? What are they?
3. Suggest ways of understanding children's needs, and say why you think this is important.

1. J. Flavel: *The Character of a True Evangelical Pastor* pp. 568–9.

7.
Teaching whom?—The child's needs

It is not the purpose of this chapter to rehearse the spiritual needs of the child, since this has been done earlier. Rather, we need to grapple with the sheer demands of teaching, recognizing the needs of the recipients, the children. We need to remind ourselves of all that has been said about befriending the children and getting to know them at the personal level, both in and out of class. Prospective teachers must remind themselves that there is no 'average' child. The members of their class are not peas in a pod. Some will be forthcoming, others retiring; some will be competitive, others will be content to play second fiddle. Some children will be more easily enthused than others and the child who is the 'loner' must be recognized.

The individuality of each child represents a great potential which may be harnessed for good once the teacher has gained his interest and attentiveness. If this is not achieved, the child may equally represent a vast potential for disruption and trouble. This is particularly a problem in the Sunday School situation because of the current general lack of home discipline. The Sunday School teacher has none of the powers or sanctions of the day-school teacher. There is no effective threat of punishment in the Sunday School, other than that of excluding the child altogether. This the teacher will obviously be most reluctant to do.

It is important to repeat at this point that teaching is all about relationship; that is to say, no teaching can take place unless the proper roles of teacher and taught are both willingly accepted by the child. This will not be achieved by a kind of 'chumminess'. Children are not impressed by this. Where the right relationship exists there will be a right discipline – not in the negative sense, but rather the discipline of an ordered environment. Children prefer the teacher to be in charge and enjoy the security of familiarity and order. If the disruption of this order by unruly children is allowed to persist, confidence in the teacher will soon evaporate and milder children will be hindered and possibly stop coming. In extreme cases, therefore, the final option of refusing admission to an unruly child must be exercised.

At this point there is another serious danger, that of becoming preoccupied with the difficult child. Sometimes the teacher's attention is utterly taken up by the uncontrollable, incorrigible child, or engaged by the attractive rogue, so that the more timid, meek, shy, or simply rather colourless child becomes neglected.

By now any prospective teachers may be thinking that it is all so complicated and there are so many points to watch out for, that it is all too much to cope with. Do not despair! Many of the hints being given are elementary and with a little experience will become 'second nature'. There is a kind of 'knack' or 'touch' to teaching, which some people seem to have by nature, but others can also acquire by good technique and experience.

In the teaching profession there is a saying that 'Teachers are born, not trained.' This is certainly true of those we might call 'great natural teachers'. At the other extreme there are those who are never going to be teachers, on account of their temperament, and no amount of training, nor even the possession of a teaching diploma, will alter the fact. Such people will experience only stress and misery if they persist. Between these two extremes there are the great mass of professional teachers who, by training and application, can develop what may be quite meagre natural aptitudes, to become most competent teachers.

In the same way, the Sunday School teacher, by disciplined application, can develop what might appear to be only a meagre gift to a degree of great usefulness in the Lord's service. However, in the realm of teaching the Word of God, there is another factor, namely the work of the Holy Spirit. The most competent teacher with a great natural aptitude can achieve no spiritual result apart from the ministry of the Holy Spirit. In fact, the goal is infinitely more likely to be achieved by someone with a meagre gift in dependence upon the Holy Spirit than by the 'great teacher' who does not seek the help of the Spirit.

Whatever the degree of gift or talent, the teacher must proceed in conscious dependence upon the Holy Spirit. To attend training sessions, to examine one's methods and progress or to share in teachers' meetings is not to minimize the need for the work of the Holy Spirit. He is not quenched or grieved by a grasp and use of wise teaching methods. The Holy Spirit is no more dishonoured by the teacher learning a few laws of teaching than he is grounded by the law of gravity! We need to look briefly together at seven laws of teaching.

1. The law of the teacher

The teacher must be someone who knows the lesson, truth

or art to be taught. This is a good starting-point — not methods, but message. The Sunday School teacher must aim at being thoroughly familiar with the Word of God. This covers the general subject. Each lesson, however, must be thoroughly grasped; the teacher should know *more* than he has time to teach, not just enough to fill up the lesson time.

2. The law of the pupil

The pupil is one who attends with interest to the lesson. Do not try to teach without the attention of the child. Never speak to the child without his looking directly at you. Never begin to address a group of children until you have the undivided attention of each of them. Do not continue speaking to them if they stop looking at you. To begin with you may think that you sound a 'nag' to your children, but if you do not demand this attention all your subsequent attempts to teach will be wasted. If you are prepared to speak to children who are not ready either to listen or to look at you, they will assume that what you are saying is not very important or that you do not particularly care. If you demand their attention they will soon learn to give it and will realize from your earnestness the importance of what you are about to say to them. 'Get the children's attention. If they do not hearken, you may talk, but you will speak to no purpose whatever. If they do not listen you can go through your labours as an unmeaning drudgery to yourselves and your pupils too. You can do nothing without securing their attention.'[1]

3. The law of language

Language is used as the medium between teacher and learner, and must be common to both. In the class you have the teacher, with his fund of knowledge and experience, and the children, with their potential of interest and attentiveness. The vital next step is successful communication between them. As words are the normal way of communicating, the teacher will need to use language which makes sense to the child. To do this, the teacher should remember to
   a. Study carefully their language, listen to their conversation before Sunday School.
   b. Use short sentences of the simplest construction.
   c. Illustrate the meaning of new words, perhaps using a story or visual aid.

4. The law of the lesson

The lesson to be mastered must be explicable in terms of the truth already known by the learner — the unknown must be explained by means of the known. This is fundamental to all successful teaching. You can only teach new truths by fastening them on to what is already known. This was the method used by the Lord Jesus Christ — for example, his references to Old Testament people and events and to nature. Your lesson must be pre-digested and capable of being expressed in your own terms. Unless you really know it, how will you explain it to your children? The folly of simply reading out a lesson from a book is no more apparent than at this point.

5. The law of the teaching process

The teaching process is the arousal and use of the pupil's mind to grasp the desired thought. This is closely linked with the previous paragraph, except that now we are striving to get the child to discover the truth for himself. This can be done by providing him with something to think about, that is, implanting truths which we can draw out at a future time. We also need to ask ceaseless questions, for questioning is more than a teaching device; it leads to the discovery of truth. In turn we also need to provoke questions in the mind of the child. We ought to be discontented until the pupils are asking, 'Who? When? Why? Where? How?'

6. The law of the learning process

The learning process is that of thinking a new idea or truth into one's own understanding. The means for this are reproduction, interpretation and application.

Reproduction is being able to restate a lesson by committing it to memory. This is good, but does not necessarily mean that the lesson is understood.

Interpretation adds the 'Why?' to the 'What?' The child has to be able to state his actual understanding of the lesson.

Application to life is the acid test of a lesson fully learned. We aim for much more than a head-knowledge of the truth. We must not be satisfied if the child only expresses an opinion; we must encourage the practice of what is preached.

7. The law of review and application

Review and application are the test and proof of effective teaching. Review, rethink, reknow, reproduce and apply the material that has been taught. This is the great value of a series of lessons within a structured syllabus pursued by the whole Sunday School. The review, reinforcement and application of the previous lesson can form a valuable part of the present one.

For further study
1. Memorize the seven laws of teaching.
2. How does a teacher develop interest? Name at least four things that affect interest.
3. Could the appearance of the teacher's manual in the class impress the pupils? Give reasons for your answer.

1. C.H. Spurgeon. 'Lecture on Attention', *Lectures to My Students*, Marshall, Morgan & Scott, p. 127.

8.
With what?—The materials and aids

In the next chapter we shall come to the question of lesson preparation, but it seems right at this moment to pause and consider the various materials that are available as aids for the Sunday School teacher. We need to remember at the outset that an aid is not an end in itself. It is a means of improving our instruction of the children. The teacher must not become the slave of the aid, nor must his lesson book become the be-all and end-all of what he is about. Aids to Sunday School teaching are available under the following categories: (1) teachers' manuals; (2) visual aids; (3) handcraft materials.

1. Teachers' manuals

The whole question of using a teacher's manual is a vexed one. There are so many choices available, of varying quality of production. Unhappily the quality of the contents does not always go hand in hand with the quality of the presentation. Let us try to guide a choice by the process of elimination.

A common fault with many Sunday School teachers' manuals is that they do practically everything for the teacher. Everything is mapped out, from the beginning to the end of the Sunday School, and the lesson is included, ready made. This may be one reason why the 'glossy' attractive books, with their accompanying pupil workbooks, are so popular. Where Sunday School teaching is undertaken by young and immature Christians, the easy option of this kind of book is virtually irresistible.

A second fault is that publishers tend to be very rigid. The teacher must not become the slave of a rigid syllabus, timetable or lesson manual. In some of the products, for example, unless the prescribed lesson is exactly taught, then the children's take-home material becomes largely irrelevant. Another fault is that this take-home material is itself often so well produced and so complete that either the child is inhibited from working on the sheet, or there is simply nothing for him to do on it. He can take it home and his mother or father may or may not read it to him. A parallel failure can be identified — namely, that the contents of a take-home leaflet are very often not Bible-centred. Leaflets which encourage children to open their Bibles, find a passage and do some work by way of discovery are much better. Consequently, as the Sunday School syllabus is to be Bible-centred rather than child-centred or situation-centred, so the lesson is to be Bible-centred rather than manual-centred.

The best teachers' manuals are those which set out to work through a given area of biblical material over a specified period. They should provide study notes to help the teacher understand the passage and identify its main aim and to enable him to produce his own lesson. The lesson aim may thus be pursued with great flexibility and individuality. Equally the take-home leaflets should reinforce the contents of the Bible passage involved rather than regurgitate the contents of the lesson manual. We want the children to work on the Bible, not on a book. The leaflets will thus be suitable for a variety of teachers, with a variety of emphases in their own lessons.

The value of helpful manuals is precisely that the teacher is guided over a long period and can be sure that a good balance of biblical material is being covered. Each section and each lesson will thus be seen and taught in its inter-relatedness to the whole. Another value of manuals which take the form of a study guide to the teacher is that they provide helpful insights, knowledge and the experience of those who may have spent a lifetime in such work and have a wealth of ideas to share with others. The lesson manual is to the teacher what the good commentary is to the preacher — which is not to say that teachers should not use commentaries!

These criteria seem to be met by such manuals as *Go Teach* publications, for example. Let the teacher be warned that this approach demands more dedication and more perspiration than ready-made lessons. Perhaps this is a reason why it is not so popular with some. However, these manuals do provide for each lesson a suggested outline to help the teacher who otherwise might really be stumped for ideas. Use the teacher's manual to prepare the lesson and then leave it at home.

2. Visual aids

There are a wide variety of visual aids available on the market and it would be sensible if every Sunday School could delegate one of its teachers to make himself an expert in this field. At least a list of publishers and a collection of their catalogues ought to be available. At quarterly teachers' meetings, when the new set of lesson material has arrived, a useful planning evening could include an examination of the materials available for any given series or lesson. Necessary arrangements can then be made to purchase or hire in good time.

If it is true that children remember 24% of what they hear, 46% of what they see and 89% of what they both hear and see, then the judicious use of visual aids is clearly beneficial. But we need to sound some notes of warning.

a. Limitations of visual aids

One of the great arguments for the use of visual aids is that Christ himself used them. The idea is that when he was preaching on the parable of the sower, for example, he directed the gaze of his hearers across the landscape to such a person actually at work. This, of course, is entire conjecture. On only one occasion did our Lord definitely use a visual aid. Even then the exercise was more of an object lesson than the use of a visual aid. It was when he said, 'Show me a penny.' What Christ generally did in his teaching, by his expert use of parable, was to create a mental image in the minds of his hearers by the use of words. This is the ideal. The teacher who has this ability has a very great gift. Vivid impressions thus created remain long and deeply in the memory. Let us not be over-committed to the value of the visual aid. We live in an age when 'eye gate' is over-rated. The advent of T.V. and more visual and active methods of teaching in school are producing a generation unable to sit and listen for any length of time. And yet it is through verbal communication that the gospel is mainly to be conveyed. 'Faith comes from hearing the message, and the message is heard through the Word of Christ.'

In this respect we should also remember the danger that

an elaborate visual aid may be so elaborate and striking that *it alone* remains in the memory. With the best visual aid there has to be some verbal application of its message, and under the engaging impact of the aid itself this application can very easily be lost. How often has the child remembered the teacher's illustration, picture or joke, but entirely forgotten its application?

b. Complications of visual aids

The best visual aids are the simplest ones. Again, the visual aids which the teacher will manipulate best are the ones he has devised himself. Such aids emerge from his own grasp and understanding of the subject matter. The lesson has been thought through and his imagination has been engaged. Thus the purpose and aim of the aid is thoroughly grasped and its purpose delimited in the mind of the teacher. Beware of elaborate, complicated, commercial aids. It is easy for the teacher to become so encumbered with the apparatus that his zeal for, and grasp of, the lesson can be lost. Elaborate pictures may inhibit children, especially if they are to be copied. Even the artistic Philistine can draw matchstick men, and children are able to copy these figures and enjoy doing so. In the production of visual aids, it is important for the teacher to be himself.

Having uttered these warnings, let us be aware of the vast array of materials which are now available to us, from maps, charts, wall pictures, flash cards, to the more sophisticated slide, film strip, sound strip, or overhead projector. If these are to be employed, the use of them must be rehearsed and mastered and the apparatus must be set up *before* the lesson begins. A perusal of materials available will suffice to teach the need to be highly selective in the use of aids of mixed quality or content.

3. Handcraft materials

Some subjects are more susceptible to handcraft activity than others. Suppose, for example, the series for the next few weeks is about the tabernacle built by the Israelites in the desert. Week by week the lessons are going to describe various parts and pieces belonging to the tabernacle. Imagine the dullness if the teacher simply sits and describes, week in week out, one item after another. No pictures, no slides, no models. Will the children have a mental picture of the tabernacle? The tabernacle was built in order to be a visual representation of the gospel. Why not give them such a visual representation? What better than to build the series of lessons around a project in which week by week the tabernacle is actually built up by the class in a model form? Cardboard boxes, matchboxes, old curtain materials etc. all provide a good stock of materials that could be kept in hand. Teachers should be on the look-out for such ideas and projects. However, the model or the handcraft is still only an aid. It is not an end in itself, but a vehicle for the communication of a lesson. Again teachers must be themselves in this respect and not attempt more than they can cope with. Do not embark on the construction of a model until you have previously tested out your ideas and know that they will work.

For further study

1. Define the purpose of an aid.
2. Do you think aids can ever hinder teaching? If so, how?
3. If you were asked by your Sunday School to be the visual aids expert, what would you do to be of most help to your colleagues?
4. Make a list of Bible objects or places that you think might be suitable for model-making or handcraft work.

9.
How?—The preparation of the lesson

Introduction

It cannot be over-stressed that it is only the bad teacher who begins lesson preparation at the last minute — perhaps as late as Sunday lunch-time for the class to be taught that same afternoon. The bad teacher thus finds it necessary to arrive at lesson time with the teacher's manual still in his hands, instead of in his heart and his head! The bad teacher has spent no time during the week looking for apt illustrations. Neither has he studied each individual verse mentioned in the manual, nor allowed the Holy Spirit to lead him into Scriptures which are not even mentioned in the lesson book. The bad teacher will thus be hesitant, repetitive and stale, because he will be reduced to mouthing well-worn jargon! These are perils to be avoided by all who feel called of God to this work. 'Do your best to present yourself to God as one approved, a workman who does not need to be ashamed and who correctly handles the word of truth' (2 Tim.2:15).

We shall consider the matter of lesson preparation under four main headings.

1. General preparation

We need to remind ourselves at this point of all that has been said about the character of the Sunday School teacher (see chapter 4 on 'Who should teach?'). The general preparation of the Sunday School teacher is found within the spiritual life of the dedicated Christian. The teacher must prepare himself before he prepares any lessons. This is accomplished by his lifelong regular habits of Bible reading and prayer. Of course, in all of this the teacher should always be on the look-out for material to help him in his Sunday School teaching. This will apply especially to his Bible reading. The Bible should be read in two ways.

a. *The study of a short passage.* A few verses at a time are studied in depth and the contents are made the subject of meditation by asking questions to establish the meaning of the text.

b. *Reading straight through.* The Bible ought to be read, equally, chapters at a time and sometimes a book at a time. In this way the teacher will develop a mental map of the ground covered by the Bible. He will be better able to relate particular stories to the whole as this map becomes imprinted upon his mind. Another part of the teacher's preparation of himself is his background reading of other books. The regular reading of Christian biographies and church history will provide an ample store of those stories which he will need to enliven his lessons when they tend to become heavy or dull. Always read with a notebook and make an index of helpful and arresting stories under various topical headings.

2. Detailed preparation

The following points are meant to be guides to the enjoyable and effective preparation of Sunday School lessons.

1. *Make a beginning.* Start as early in the week as possible. It is a good idea to read the passage and the lesson aim for the following Sunday on the Sunday evening before. It will be lodged in the memory and throughout the week the mind may work subconsciously. As the ideas surface from time to time throughout the week make a note of anything which might be useful in your preparation. With the lesson in mind a teacher might glean much from his own private devotions and incidents in his daily life which would otherwise be forgotten if the lesson had not been perused early.

2. *Set aside definite periods* each week for the actual compilation of the lesson. Do not allow this time to be usurped. When you come to this period have your Bible, lesson book, any commentaries or Bible dictionaries you may possess and writing materials to hand. If you have any other versions of the Bible apart from the one you use, put them ready also.

3. *Start in prayer* and ask the Holy Spirit to guide your study. Tell him you are depending completely upon his help, and that you want a message from the Lord for your class on Sunday.

4. *Turn to your lesson book.* Do not read the lesson material yet. Simply make a note of the Scripture passage, close the book and turn to the Bible. Read the passage through a number of times. While you are doing this expect the Holy Spirit to impress important truths upon your mind. These truths will be the main points of your lesson. They may not always emerge immediately.

5. *Find the central truth* of the passage and what its

effect ought to be in the lives of your hearers. A good method to find the meaning of a passage is to ask questions.

i. Start with general questions

The following is a list of suggested questions with which to begin in order to get at the meaning of a passage:

'Why is this story here at all?'

'Why is it in this book, in this place in this book?'

'What is the setting, historically and geographically?'

'Why is the story told in this particular way?'

Make a note of each question you ask and the answer or possible answers. (*How* the Bible says things can be almost as informative as *what* it says.) Check your answers against other parts of the Bible. Be aware of parallel passages (e.g. Kings and Chronicles, Exodus and Numbers or Deuteronomy, the four Gospels). The way the story is told in one book may throw light on the same story told in a slightly different way in another. It is of interest, for example, to know why Mark gives us an account of an incident in a different way to Matthew. What was his purpose? To discover the answer to some of these questions you will need to consult a concordance and a Bible commentary.

ii. Then ask more detailed questions

Consider the following examples:

'What is the exact meaning of this paragraph, or text, or word?'

'What did this word originally mean?'

'Where else does it occur?'

'Why use this word and not another?'

Do as much as you can to get 'under the skin' of a passage. Think! Nothing will help you to master the content of the Bible more thoroughly than a process like this. Obviously the use of concordances, Bible dictionaries and commentaries comes in here. A list of helpful books will be given at the end.

iii. Questions about content

Try the following as examples of questions to discover the content of the passage:

'What is the truth being taught?'

'Is it being taught directly or incidentally?'

'If incidentally, is there a passage of the Bible which teaches the same truth more clearly?'

'Is this a teaching passage?'

'If so, is there a Bible story which will illuminate it for the children?'

'Is it a story?'

'If so, is there a text which will "fix" the truth implied?'

This is all to say that we must constantly be trying to find doctrines from the text. It is a method to draw out what is in there. It is called 'exposition'. Even Sunday School teaching must be simple exposition. Beware of coming to a passage with a doctrine already in mind. That is imposition! Do not construct a doctrine or a lesson by leaping from one isolated text to another. That is gymnastics!

All this, of course, presupposes a working knowledge of basic Christian doctrine. But do not be discouraged, because you will find that the process of preparation will actually increase and broaden your knowledge of Christian doctrine. There are some simple doctrinal reference books which will help the teacher to identify doctrines and to check his own understanding of the use of certain texts. (A word of warning here. Do not trust the references given in books. Always look them up. You will be surprised how many misprints there are and how many of the texts given do not immediately appear to support the doctrine propounded!).

6. *Think of the pupil.* Try to see how the truths discovered can be conveyed and applied to the pupils. Make sure at this point that you know the aim of the lesson. Here you may need to ask another set of questions of a more practical kind. These should seek to discover the best way to present this theme to the children. Try to fix on a definite theme for your lesson. Write it down in front of you in a sentence. For example, 'In this lesson I wish to teach the children . . .' This is your aim. Pray over it. Is it important, vital, true? Can you deliver that message to your children? If so, then decide on how much material in the passage is necessary to support your aim. *Use only that material which is necessary!* Do not show off. Do not think that you have to display your vast array of knowledge. Most of what you have studied is not for the children; it is for you. Don't say, 'What a pity not to tell them this little gem, or that, which I have just this minute discovered!' It is better to digest your discovery for a week or two and put it to the test. Be ruthless. Omit all that does not directly contribute to that aim which you feel God has shown you in your study.

The time has now come to get down on paper a written lesson outline.

7. *Determine the conclusion.* This must come first. It comes last in your lesson, but it is the first thing you make notes on. It needs much careful thought. It is there to summarize and focus your whole lesson and to bring it to bear upon the hearer. It should express and apply in a final sentence or two the whole aim of your lesson. Having decided the theme and the aim, write down the conclusion, how you wish to express it and apply it to the hearers. This is the impression you want to create in the child's mind.

Here is the truth you want your class to take away with them. Do this first. Make sure it represents the main thrust of the Bible passage. When you have accomplished this, make sure the main body of your lesson leads directly to it. This will help you in the next step.

8. *Determine your subject matter.* Now try to arrange an outline of headings, working logically, step by step, towards your goal. The method will vary with the lesson, depending on the nature of the material. It might consist of facets of the truth under headings, of stages in a story told in sequence, or of ingredients in a situation which together make up a whole picture. Make sure that your outline fits the Bible material and not vice versa. Beware of the danger of alliterated headings. The temptation to have a series of headings which sound the same, or which rhyme, is very great. Of course, if you can do it successfully, it helps to fix the material of the lesson in the mind. But the temptation is to bend the contents of the Bible passage to suit your headings. Last, and perhaps most difficult of all, as you are building up your subject matter, ask questions about application as you go along. These may be numerous. Select the really important ones. It is here that you will become relevant or irrelevant to your children. Illustrations will come into your thinking at this point.

You may find it advisable to apply the lesson as you go along in some respects, rather than leaving all the application as the 'grand finale'. The same application can be given in different ways. Make sure, however, that at the end it is the main point that is left as the abiding impression.

9. *Determine the introduction.* How you introduce your material is most vital. The introduction has to be arresting. The interest of the pupils has to be engaged from the very beginning. Although the introduction comes first in your

lesson it comes last in your preparation. Remember, you cannot decide your introduction until you have decided your theme. You must know what it is you are going to introduce before you introduce it. Think of it in terms of a journey. The destination has to be decided upon first. Then you choose a route. It is only then that you can select the direction in which you set out. The introduction and method should vary each week, making use, for example, of visual aids, revision or incidents which have occurred during the week.

10. *Summary*. In working out your actual lesson outline a good plan to employ is as follows:

  i. Decide the lesson aim and write it out.

 ii. Write out the conclusion, the actual goal of the lesson.

iii. Arrange lesson headings to lead to that goal. Check that the series of headings actually proceeds smoothly into your conclusion; the body must be attached to the tail.

iv. Develop and write out the body of your lesson. Do not forget to teach the story in an interesting way, inserting applications as you go along, using parallel Bible passages and other material for illustration.

 v. Work on the introduction and make it as engaging as you can.

It is not a bad discipline to write out your lesson in full. This is especially true if you are a beginner at Sunday School teaching. It will help you to clarify your thoughts, fix your mode of expression, check any difficult vocabulary and impress your lesson and its structure upon your memory. This manuscript is not for you to read in class. It is not even for you to commit verbatim to memory. It is simply to help you form your lesson. Make notes of headings from your outline and take these into the lesson with you as your only written aid. Trust the Lord to give you an immediate and lively presentation of what you have studied and written out. You may find it necessary to have at least your conclusion written out word for word, so that you can be absolutely sure that you have not been diverted from your aim and that as you come to a close, you have expressed precisely the truth that you want them to get.

3. Use of study aids

The guidelines given above have not taken any account of the Sunday School lesson manual. The use of these aids comes into consideration now. Let us put their use in the form of several general rules.

1. Get as much out of the passage as you can for yourself before reading what the contributor to the lesson manual has written. If you read what the lesson book says first, you may find that the contributor's ideas effectively jam your own thinking. This operates in the same way that a T.V. is affected when an unsuppressed vehicle goes by. The screen is blotted out by a mass of 'snow' and we cannot see the T.V. picture. The same thing will happen to the teacher who rushes straight to the lesson book and lesson outline, before doing his or her own work. The unsuppressed ideas of others can effectively prevent you getting your own view of the subject. If the lesson book provides notes to help you in your study of the passage then you could use these at an early stage of your study.

2. After you have exhausted your own ideas, use whatever commentaries and Bible helps you may have. Read these and the manual carefully and include with your own material any fresh thoughts which will enrich your lesson.

Take full advantage of the wisdom and spiritual insight of others who have also carefully considered the message for boys and girls from the Scripture passage you have studied.
3.   If your thoughts do not gel into a clear lesson aim and outline, then the lesson book may come to your help. But even in the use of the suggested lesson outline, do not be slavish. If the lesson outline in the book has the effect of priming your own pump, then make use of it to prompt your own thoughts to flow. If this happens, put the manual aside again. It has served its purpose for the time being.
4.   The lesson book may provide you, when all other efforts have been exhausted, with the only viable lesson you can think of. If so, then use it. That is what it is for. Many a preacher has been glad as a last resort to base a sermon outline on something he has read. There is no shame in that. What does any of us have which we have not received? Please do not take this as an excuse merely to pick up the book every week to 'parrot off' the written lesson! If you do that, your children will quickly become very bored.

Needless to say, if you have to use the lesson outline suggested, then do your own work on it as before and make your own lesson notes from it. Never, never, merely take your book to Sunday School to read the lesson out of it. It should never be necessary to take the lesson manual into the class-room at all.

4. The importance of prayer

Stop and kneel in the presence of the Lord if at any time in your preparation you feel unable to perceive or receive a message from the Lord. Ask him to show you anything hindering the work of his Spirit. Confess it and repeat your dependence upon him. Pray earnestly that, by whatever means, the Lord will give you a lesson to bring to your children next Sunday. And if and when he does, even if it is by the use of the lesson outline in the manual as a last resort, then kneel and worship the Lord. Thank him for his grace and ask him to make you lively in the delivery of your lesson and a living illustration of it, so that your children can see and hear the message from God.

For further study:
1. Suggest a list of headings for a topical index to make notes on Bible readings.
2. Memorize the ten steps given in the detailed preparation.
3. What are the four rules given about using the lesson manual?

10.
What shall we do?— The conduct of the Sunday School

Everything that is done during the Sunday School hour should be geared to the presentation of the lesson. Think of an arrow. The arrowhead is the lesson; the shaft is the whole Sunday School hour. The flights on the arrow represent the direction of the Sunday School hour. The whole must be aimed at the mark for which the lesson has been prepared.

This hour is vital. How foolish it is to approach it casually! It must be prepared carefully and in detail by the leader for the day. (Do not assume that this must always be the superintendent.) Consider for a moment how vital this one hour is. It must be made to count.

A child's week consists of 168 hours. The child will spend, on average,

> 70 hours — in bed
> 30 hours — at school
> 10 hours — at the table
> 20 hours — watching T.V.!
> 38 hours — for everything else

Of those thirty-eight the Sunday School teacher has but one hour! It is right to concentrate on that hour to make it as effective as we can. The teacher must bend mind, imagination and all his talents to the content and the time-

table of that one hour. In that one hour the work of
eternity has to be done. The following is a suggested
approach to the timetable and contents of that hour.

1. Teachers must be early

The teacher must arrive early enough to have his room or
teaching area ready before the children arrive. Tables, chairs,
books, materials — all must be set out before the first child
arrives. The first child might be five minutes early and the
teacher must be prepared for that. At the very least, the
teacher ought to arrive fifteen minutes before the official
starting-time. If he does not, he will be late. The writer well
remembers his first experience as a primary school teacher,
when he arrived five minutes before the school bell sounded
and was reprimanded by his headmaster for being late! The
headmaster was right. This rule may sound legalistic and
hard, but if it is not observed the teacher will not be ready
for the children when they arrive. The teacher needs to be
composed and unoccupied in order to greet them, to chat
to them and listen to their news. He must have the appearance of having all the time in the world, especially if a
parent turns up with a problem. It is obvious that the
teacher cannot give that impression while he is busy doing
something else. He has only one hour! That hour must be
entirely for the children. 'Do not bother me for a minute or
two,' says the unprepared teacher, 'I am just getting ready
for my class.' These are precious minutes which belong to
the child. And the teacher has only one hour in the whole
week to do a work for eternity. Give the child the whole
hour. Arrive early. Be prepared.

A teacher who is late is not only letting down the whole

team and the Sunday School, but he is also letting down the Lord. The Christian's approach must be one of 'making the most of every opportunity, because the days are evil' (Eph. 5:16). We must be in earnest. One hour! We need every minute of it.

2. Punctuality

The first part of the Sunday School must begin and end promptly, otherwise the teachers will not have time to complete their lessons. Inevitably that part of the lesson which is the most important will suffer, namely, the last part, which is intended to create the impression which the teacher wishes to remain with the child. So the whole climax of the lesson and thus of the Sunday School can be lost because of a hurried closure of the lesson. Too easily this time can be lost in the first ten minutes of the Sunday School. It is good for the Sunday School to have an agreed timetable to which all must endeavour to adhere. Not counting those informal minutes with the children before the official starting-time, the following timetable is a basic suggestion.

    a. *Registration* including time for informal chat in classes   5 minutes

    b. *Opening period* – whole school   15–20 minutes

    c. *Lesson time* – in classes   25–30 minutes

    d. *Short closing assembly*   5 minutes

This leaves five minutes leeway for moving about and the odd encroachment.

3. The opening part

What should occupy us in this fifteen to twenty minutes of the opening? Is it to be a time of formal worship? It ought to be a time of worship and interest, stimulating the children and preparing for the lesson to follow. The worship must not be stuffy or dull. It must not be conceived of in terms of the same kind of content as, for example, the morning service.

Hymn singing is problematic. Not many children know many hymns. It is better to sing one or two verses that are known and that can be sung well, than to pound meaninglessly right through a hymn. A single verse could be sung several times during the course of the Sunday School and be repeated at the end. This will help to extend the repertoire. The language of hymns also presents us with a problem. The classic hymns of Christianity are largely couched in a language which is unfamiliar to contemporary children. This does not mean that they are out of date, but it might mean that they are unsuitable as introductions to worship for such children. If the language manifestly needs a lot of explanation it might be better not to sing a given hymn, but to choose something more contemporary. The children can always graduate to Isaac Watts a little later on.

Choruses can be used, but with care. They should not be used for a mere singsong. The choice of them could contribute to the theme of the lesson.

Prayer can be a part of the opening worship, but it must be relevant to the children and to what they know of the Sunday School or any missionary contacts which the Sunday School has. It may encompass all the normal needs of human life and family situations with which the children will be familiar.

The Bible reading should not be too long and ought to be relevant to the theme of the lesson to follow. A number of variations in the manner of Bible reading can be employed. The teacher must always be on the look-out for stimuli to prod the children's attention to the Bible reading.

Memory work of various kinds can be included in this time. Memory verses from the Bible can be taught and tested in a variety of ways. These may be a means of recapitulating previous work. Here the leader must take care to be imaginative, fresh, lively and interesting. The recall of lessons or memory verses could be made more like a quiz. Any number of T.V. formats will be readily recognizable to the children. They will respond better to this than to something which resembles a school test. Make sure that some of the questions are well within the ability of the youngest or slowest children in the school to answer. Make a habit of asking the youngest person whose hand is up to answer the question, and never get into the habit of asking the first with a hand up. Do not allow the calling out of answers, as this may destroy the purpose of your questions and undermine the discipline of the school.

Revision is also important and may be conducted in various ways. Always seek to reward good work. Always try to ask a child a question it can answer, so that the child will succeed and feel rewarded. Endeavour to find something to encourage the dullest pupil. Before you embark on any necessary correction, try to find something for which to give praise, however slight. The whole matter of reward is very difficult. Teachers should reward effort rather than achievement, on the principle that a child can do no more than his or her best, however limited the attainment might be. Some children are not as bright as others, but it is not our business to demonstrate it. Remember that encouragement goes a very long way. Do you remember the Aesop fable about the traveller and the sun and the wind? The sun and the wind had a competition to see who could get the traveller's cloak off his back the quickest. The more the wind howled, the tighter the traveller clung to his cloak, but as soon as the sun shone warmly on him he peeled it off by himself. Let them feel the warmth of your encouragement and they will respond most readily.

Children who are regularly and publicly reprimanded or made examples of, and who become the butt of everyone else's mirth will be discouraged and humiliated. They will show what they think of the Sunday School and the teacher by never turning up again. Sunday School is not compulsory, nor do we wish it so to be. The compulsory teaching of religious knowledge in day schools has become a very effective barrier for countless thousands of children to their encountering a true and warm representation of the Christian gospel. The compulsory nature of it has acted like a most effective innoculation against the real thing. We do not want Sunday School to be compulsory. We want the children to want to come. Therefore just as far as credibility permits, be positively encouraging to every child. Let them feel that Sunday School, especially this open part, is a great pleasure. Let it be really enjoyable; make it fun; make it interesting. You may feel sometimes that you are in charge of a herd of small donkeys. Very well, remember that the carrot is more effective than the stick! The promotion of Sunday School and the interest in the first part can be enhanced by the use of badges, charts and competitions, but far and away the most effective means of stimulating interest is the enthusiasm of the teachers.

Different teachers may have different ideas. These should be pooled and discussed at regular teachers' meetings, as should the planning of the leading of the first part of Sunday School. Both planning and leading should be shared among all who are involved.

There are two postscripts to add to this section.

a. Co-operation

The leader of the open part of Sunday School, whoever he is, needs the co-operation of all the other teachers. Every teacher ought to be totally involved in what is going on. Each teacher should sit with his class and should prompt and encourage them. Teachers themselves can take part. If the leader wishes to make a fool of anyone, in fun, let it be another teacher. A disinterested teacher, or one wandering about like a lost sheep, or arranging his own class area because he has arrived late, is most effectively working against the interest of the whole school. He is in fact saying, 'I don't really care.' This one hour is all that is available. 'I care' says, 'Sixty minutes to the hour.' A group of teachers having a discussion in the corner is as unhelpful as a distraction from outside, or even more so.

b. Discipline

Teachers can help one another by co-operating in the matter of discipline. It is surprising how often Sunday School teachers make elementary mistakes in the matter of discipline. Fundamental to the whole matter of discipline is the development by the teacher of a kind of 'presence'. By 'presence' I mean that when the teacher arrives among a group of children his very presence affects them. Simply because the teacher is there the child must know that misbehaviour, indifference or inattention are not permissible. It is helpful if there can be a pattern of behaviour which is acceptable to all the teachers. The school will benefit from a consistent application of those things which are tolerable and those which are not. This will establish a pattern which the children will rapidly recognize and accept. Let them know what the teachers together expect by way of behaviour and attention, and never proceed until it is obtained. (At this point it might be helpful to read again the comments made about discipline in chapter 7.)

Good discipline begins with a purposeful, ordered, interesting programme. Unoccupied children are potentially disruptive. If you believe in your programme, then insist that the children involve themselves in it. But before you put your faith in your programme, make sure that you have a programme which justifies your faith in it!

4. The last five minutes

A variety of interesting activities can clamour for the occupation of this precious time. If the children have a points system or competition for such things as attendance and bringing the Bible, they can be shown their performances by means of a visual aid. This information will have been collated by the superintendent from the registers completed earlier. Notice of specially important matters can be impressed upon the children. Another brief review of a previous memory text, or a salient point in the lesson, can be undertaken. Suggestions can be made for activities or items to be brought for the following week. Final instructions can be given about the completion of the take-home leaflet. Try to make the Sunday School close with an exciting, unanimous activity, so that the children leave sorry that the time has come to an end.

Conclusion

The Sunday School teacher has only one hour out of a child's total waking week of ninety-seven hours. One hour a week! If a child comes to Sunday School for thirty weeks out of the fifty-four, then the Sunday School teacher in that year only has him for as long as he spends at day school in one week. Consider it this way: the Sunday School teacher needs to have the average child in his class for twenty weeks before he can compete even approximately to the time that child spends in front of the T.V. in one week. Any Sunday School leader or teacher who does not know how to fill that hour, or is not adequately prepared for that hour, or merely packs it out with time-fillers, ought to ask himself again, and make sure of the answer to this very basic question, about his calling to and competence for this work.

The teacher has so much to cram into one hour. At this point let it be said that the use of time to prepare special items, playlets, recitations and singing for a parents' afternoon or a Sunday School anniversary has to be kept strictly under control. Such things can legitimately have a place in the opening part of Sunday School, but if, for weeks on end, they become the be-all and end-all of the Sunday School, then they have become an indefensible waste of time. What is the point of allowing six weeks' lessons to go by the board, simply to put on a show for the parents? It is much better to work imaginatively in Sunday School week by week at the lessons, producing leaflets, models etc., which can be shown to the parents, which will more fully reflect the weekly activities and which will equally contribute to the purpose of the Sunday School, namely teaching the Scripture.

Be imaginative and lively. Vary the activity. Pursue the present activity with conviction and zeal. Do it for a limited time, say for a few minutes only. Make every minute count. Then, before the interest flags, do the next thing with equal zeal and commitment. Make full use of this one hour that God has given us, in which he might transform a child for a lifetime of service, to say nothing of an eternity spent in fellowship with him.

For further study:
Plan a timetable for your Sunday School, taking into account all your local circumstances and availability of rooms, etc.

11.
How shall they hear?—The presentation of the lesson

All we have said before concerning discipline and the atmosphere in which teaching can take place needs to be underlined at this point. Good discipline begins with a well-prepared, interesting, arresting lesson. If that is what the teacher believes he has, he must not be prepared to fling it away on inattentive children. He must expect and demand their attention, win their interest and, by lively enthusiasm, endeavour to keep it. If the teacher succeeds in this, his disciplinary problems will largely be over. At this point, before we consider how to present the lesson, it is necessary to reflect on the need for an ordered and accepted relationship between the teacher and the taught. If this is not conceded, then the best of prepared lessons cannot be presented to full effect. A young and inexperienced teacher with a difficult child should, at this point, seek the help of the school leader or a more experienced teacher.

The good teacher, in prayerful dependence upon the Holy Spirit, will have prepared the lesson thoroughly. The Spirit of God will have guided the thoughts and given help in the construction of the lesson material. The earlier part of Sunday School, just concluded, should have been a help and stimulus for the teacher to deliver his lesson. Now he has a precious twenty-five minutes to sow the good seed.

The teacher's words for the next few minutes constitute the arrowhead, the point of all that Sunday School is about. The previous minutes should have given the lesson some momentum and direction, as shaft and flights to the arrow. Let the teacher remind himself silently of this and commit himself to God, praying that the arrow will find its mark.

The teacher must also depend upon the work of the Holy Spirit for the effective and fruitful presentation of his lesson. He helps in presentation as well as preparation. Only he can empower the teacher's words so that they ring true and become convincing (1 Thess. 1:5). With such help and in such confidence, the teacher must now deliver the lesson.

1. With deep personal conviction

Every Christian speaking to someone else should, in the end, simply be testifying to what he knows. The little boy who once asked C.H. Spurgeon, 'Teacher do you believe in him?' was not content with Spurgeon's repeating, 'I hope so.' He would have it, 'If you have believed in Christ, you *are* saved' (see above on page 36). The teacher must be able to speak of what he has heard, seen, tasted and handled of the good Word of life. The boy was right: there can be no true testimony except that which springs from the assured conviction of our own safety and joy in the Lord. It was a mark of our Lord's own ministry that the people marvelled at the certainty, conviction and authority with which he taught (Mark 1:27). A young teacher of religious education spent the first two years of his career in a large comprehensive school for boys. He had been sincere, but the teaching was hard and the boys apparently unresponsive. He left, thinking that he had achieved nothing. Several years later, a couple of older teenagers joined the Y.P.F. of a local church. They had previously been in this teacher's class and remembered him when his name was mentioned in the church. 'He was different,' said the boys, 'At least *he* believed it.' What an impression and effect personal conviction can have!

2. With real loving concern

No Sunday School lesson must ever be delivered in a take-it-or-leave-it attitude. The children must at least feel that the teacher wants them to believe his message. The teacher will want to be winsome and, although he may not plead with them directly all the time, yet that must be the constant attitude of his heart. This concern will go to great lengths of self-sacrifice and self-giving to the children as persons. The teacher that is in the work for the right motives must be concerned for the whole life and well-being of the child. Let the teacher remind himself of his motive at the outset.

3. With interest, variation and illustration

The teacher's own enthusiasm for his calling and his lesson will be conveyed to the children just as surely as his lack of it. Does the teacher enjoy his lesson? To face and answer that question honestly will reveal the relevance of all his preparation, the aptness of all his illustrations and the clarity of his aim. He must speak to the children as though he also lives with them in the late twentieth century, using a vocabulary which they will be able to understand. He must not use slang, nor descend to their level in that respect, but must employ good simple language. Enthusiasm and variety are vital. Some secondary school children were considering their options for the following year. The maximum size of class was to be thirty-five pupils. They were having introductory talks from various teachers about the choices available to them. Each teacher spoke about the prospects of his own subject. The following year the geography class had thirty-five pupils in it, but the economics class had only sixteen. In the ten minutes available to them one teacher had 'sold' geography; the other had not 'sold' economics. The difference was enthusiasm.

If there must be enthusiasm in the presentation, there must also be variety. If the pattern of your lesson is exactly the same, week in, week out, and the children know the kind of thing that is coming every time, then they will very soon learn to switch off. The good teacher will vary his method of presentation from week to week. Once again, success in presentation will be the result of thoughtful preparation. Consider the following variations on the structure of a lesson:

Variation 1 A. Revise
               B. Read the Scripture
               C. Tell the story
               D. Apply the lesson(s)

Variation 2 A. Tell the story
               B. Apply the lesson
               C. Work on the memory verse
               D. Summarize the lesson, using a visual aid or leaflet

Variation 3 A. Read the Scripture
              B. Quick quiz on the reading
              C. Teach the memory verse
              D. Tell the story and apply in closing

Variation 4 A. Introduce the visual aid
              B. Tell the story
              C. Apply the lesson using questions
              D. Teach the memory verse

Variation 5 A. Use the leaflet
              B. Look up the texts
              C. Complete the leaflet in stages
              D. Tell the story from leaflet
              E. Teach the memory verse

The variations are endless. Be enthusiastic and employ variety!

4. With singleness of purpose

Having planned his work carefully, the teacher must now work to this plan. There are several traps to avoid.

a. Do not be side-tracked

The teacher must beware of allowing himself too many asides and of deviating from his outline. He must beware of the real danger of fluency. The digression might be very interesting, but if it is lengthy it will use up valuable time and may result in the lesson planned not being taught. Awkward questions and interruptions will try the patience, but the teacher must learn to deal with them gently, firmly and in a way that directs the thoughts back towards the theme.

b. Do not be remote
If the teacher has contacts with his class outside of the lesson period, a friendly relationship can be established which will be invaluable during the lesson time. Present your lesson in a warm, friendly, familiar voice. Use the *same voice* you use when indulging in ordinary conversation with the children. There is no special 'steeple-in-the-throat' voice to be used for religious talk. A 'breathy' voice often conveys sentiment rather than sincerity.

c. Do not be overruled
Sometimes the children will display a strong urge to do something other than what the teacher has planned for the lesson. One or two determined children can be very difficult to control in this respect. The teacher must use his best endeavours to capture the mind and enthusiasm of the children for the lesson he has in hand. It may mean adapting the lesson plan and using the visual aid earlier than intended, or insisting upon some activity for the children, such as writing in the leaflet or following in the Bible. The teacher must always exercise his control over the direction of the lesson.

d. Do not be repetitious
The main point in any lesson must be repeated many times without the teacher appearing repetitious. An old quip about effective preaching is 'Tell them what you are going to tell them, then tell them it and finally tell them what you have told them!' In other words, the subject must be introduced, expanded and finally summarized. The art is to

say the same thing in as many different and interesting ways as possible. Bare repetition is dull.

e. Do not throw it away

Billy Bray, the famous Cornish preacher, once wanted to buy an old corner cupboard to knock into a pulpit for a chapel he had just built. The cupboard was up for sale in an auction. A stranger had given him six shillings for the auction. Billy was unfamiliar with proceedings at auctions, so when the cupboard was put up for sale he shouted, 'Here's six shillings for it. I want it for a pulpit.' 'Six shillings, going for six,' shouted the auctioneer. 'Seven,' said a voice from behind Billy. The next minute the cupboard was sold to the other bidder. Billy was foolish to bid his whole six shillings at the first go. (By the way, he eventually got the cupboard in a most wonderful way, but that is another story.)[1] It is important for the teacher not to give away all his secrets in his first two sentences. He must keep to the outline and keep his visual aids hidden until the moment he wishes to use them. It is helpful to keep some attention-catchers in reserve, to be brought out at subsequent points in the lesson. Stories and illustrations should be used at strategic points to maintain the maximum interest of the children. Involving the children with the use of Bibles or visual aids maintains attention.

f. Do not be shocked

The teacher must be prepared for almost anything that his children might say or do by way of response either to his lesson or to a question he may ask. Most children are quite untutored in the Bible and have only the most hazy and almost superstitious ideas about God, which are not improved upon by what they hear at school or see on T.V. Outrageous questions from the children must be dealt with patiently and lovingly. They ask them because they know no better and the teacher is there to teach them better. Never laugh at a child's ignorance. The teacher who does that will soon lose the confidence of that child. Sometimes a question will shake the teacher by its sheer unexpectedness or implications. When a child asks about our Lord, 'Did he have sex, Miss?' the question may be shocking to the teacher, but in the world in which the child lives and because of the permissive air which he is breathing, it may be a perfectly natural question for him to ask. The teacher must ride it comfortably with something such as, 'No Johnny, the Lord Jesus was never married. He did not come to please himself. He came because he loved us all in such a way that he had no home of his own and even left his own mother and family to give himself up entirely for our salvation.' The child has asked what to him was a perfectly reasonable question and the teacher has given a perfectly good answer.

g. *Do not over-estimate the children's capabilities*
Great care needs to be taken with the choice of vocabulary and illustrations. At this point it will be helpful to recall what has been said above about the teacher finding his or her own best age group. It will be the one into the mind of which the teacher finds it easiest to enter. For teachers who have no experience it is most important to think of elementary things. For instance, if the teacher writes on a board he must remember to use lower-case letters for children in primary school and to print his words rather than use joined-up writing. Care with the visual presentation of words is most important, especially with the younger children.

The teacher must aim at the highest and best, but to achieve it he must be down-to-earth and practical in the delivery of his lesson. He must involve all of the children in the class. He must make sure he can see every child and speak to them in a natural and clear voice. The aim is to instruct and he should do nothing to insert an element of doubt into the mind of the child. At the end the teacher must be concise and relevant in his conclusion. Above all, let every teacher remember that his children need him and that in handling the Word of life he must approach them prayerfully, spiritually and earnestly.

For further study

1. Which part of the lesson is the most vital, and why?
2. How would you find out whether a lesson has been taught successfully?
3. If there is not sufficient time to complete the lesson, should the teacher cram the remainder into the last few minutes? Or what should be done?
4. Can you remember the seven 'Don'ts' of delivering your lesson?

1. See John Tallach, *God made them great*, Banner of Truth Trust.

12.
How shall they believe?—The gospel that saves

1. The gospel that saves

This chapter is intended as a guide to all who work among children and young people and who are concerned about their salvation. It should be the ardent longing of every Sunday School teacher to see every boy and girl in their class saved by the grace of God. However, this very desire has led many astray. We must avoid the danger of over-simplification. It is easy to reduce the message to less than the gospel really is, out of a desire to simplify it for the children. There is also a great danger in the fact that children are malleable or impressionable. It is a gross violation of trust to manipulate a child to make a decision that he neither understands not truly believes in. The way of salvation is profound but not complicated. The gospel is, in fact, no different for the child than for the adult. That is to say, there are not two gospels, a mature version for grown-ups and an immature, simpler message for children. The way of salvation is simple for young and old alike. In fact, the Lord Jesus Christ said that unless men became 'as little children' they could in no way enter the kingdom of God. It is not *a special way*, but *the only way* of salvation that we shall consider together now. Children are sinners and as such need the one saving gospel of our Lord Jesus Christ. If we study the Word of God we find that salvation is spoken of in three tenses — past, present and future. This can be demonstrated by considering three Scriptures.

a. 'Not because of righteous things we had done, but because of his mercy. He saved us through the washing of rebirth and renewal by the Holy Spirit' (Titus 3:5). This indicates, by the words 'he saved us', that there is a phase of our salvation into which we enter at a definite time. This means that many believers can look back to an actual moment when they passed from death into life. Others may not know that moment, but they know they are saved, that salvation is something that happened to them in the past, once and for all.

b. 'Therefore, my dear friends, as you have always obeyed — not only in my presence, but now much more in my absence — continue to work out your salvation with fear and trembling' (Phil. 2:12). This indicates that salvation is a process which the believer is continually working out in his daily life through God's working in him.

c. 'The hour has come for you to wake up from your slumber, because our salvation is nearer now than when we first believed' (Romans 13:11). This indicates that our salvation in some sense is still future, 'because our salvation is nearer now than when we first believed'. There is a final element to salvation which will appear only when the Lord appears the 'second time, not to bear sin, but to bring salvation' (Heb. 9:28).

2. The technical terms

This three-fold way of looking at salvation is a recurring

theme in the Scriptures and can be represented by the following three terms:

1. Justification

This is the instantaneous aspect of our salvation. The believer is justified once and for all when he believes in Christ (Rom. 5:1). Justification refers to the sinner's acceptability before God. All the merits of Christ's death and life are credited to the believer the moment he trusts Christ. This is the only ground of salvation. It has been accomplished once and for all by the death of Christ upon the cross. Once a sinner is justified, he is a child of God and acceptable to God through Christ alone. This status can never be lost: 'He saved us.' Justification is not something that happens within the life of the sinner. It is the declaration of two things about the sinner by God the righteous Judge. Firstly, it is a declaration that the sinner is pardoned because all his sins have been put to Christ's account and punished there. There is thus no condemnation to those who are in Christ (Romans 8:1). Secondly, it is a declaration that the sinner has met, not only the penalty of God's law, but its requirements. He has met them in full because the righteousness of Christ, earned by his life of obedience to God's law, is put to the sinner's account (2 Cor. 5:20, 21). This transaction occurs the very instant the sinner trusts solely and simply on the Lord Jesus Christ and in his sacrificial death. This is the doctrine of justification by faith only. This is the sole ground on which a sinner may be admitted to heaven.

2. Sanctification

When a person becomes a Christian he does so because the Spirit of God has taken up residence in his heart. He begins

107

to act in a holy way. The first evidence is the exercise of faith in Christ as Saviour. This is but the beginning of a life-long process of sanctification, by which the person develops more and more spiritual fruits and becomes more and more like the Lord Jesus Christ. This life of holiness is not achieved by going back to God's law, although the Ten Commandments stand for ever as the standard of holiness God requires of us. Sanctification comes from Christ also (1 Cor. 1:30). Like everything else we receive from Christ, it is received through the exercise of faith. But it is not received instantaneously, in a lump, like justification is. No, it is received gradually, as the believer, out of love and gratitude, seeks to please his Saviour and, day by day, looks in faith to him for grace and strength to live. He has given us many means to this end, such as Bible reading, prayer, fellowship and the teaching ministry of others. It is only as Christ grows more and more within him that the believer progresses in holiness. The power of the Holy Spirit, who indwells every saved person, communicates Christ to the believer and makes this holy living possible. The Spirit takes all the benefits and power which Christ gives to the believer and applies them in his life. This is God at work in the believer as he works out his own salvation. Young Christians must be encouraged lovingly to go on looking to and living for the Lord Jesus Christ.

3. Glorification

This has to do with the future blessedness of all who are saved. One day the believer will be saved in body as well as soul. He will be delivered from all temptation and weakness and even from death itself. The new resurrection body will be incapable of sin, sickness or death. Every believer will be glorified. This is the salvation yet to come. 'Now we are the children of God, and what we will be has not yet been made known. But we know that when he appears, we shall be like him, for we shall see him as he is,' (1 John 3:2). It is this physical transformation which the apostle Paul describes in Romans 8:18-23 and which he declares to be so sure in verses 28-39 of the same chapter. It is this hope that removes the believer's fear of death and keeps him longing for the return of the Lord Jesus. Read 1 Corinthians 15, especially verses 50-58.

When we speak of the salvation of boys and girls it is exactly the salvation described above. The gospel for them is that they may be saved from sin's penalty (justification), sin's power (sanctification) and sin's presence (glorification). This salvation is received by simple childlike trust in Christ. It is much more than 'loving God', 'serving Jesus' or being 'forgiven'. We must not turn the gospel for children into babyish, sentimental nonsense. These young ones need the whole, robust truth of the gospel.

3. The fact of child conversion

When the Sunday School teacher seeks to lead a boy or girl into an experience of salvation through Christ he should bear in mind the following important points.

1. Children need to be saved
A careful study of Matthew 18 reveals the following truths:
 i. Little children are of great value in Christ's estimation (v. 5).
 ii. Little children are capable of exercising saving faith (v. 6).

iii. Little children who are heirs of salvation enjoy the same rich heritage as adult believers (v. 10).
iv. Little children are lost (vv. 11-14).[1]
 v. Little children are objects of Christ's saving work (v. 11).
vi. Little children need to be sought (v. 12).

2. *The need for regeneration, or the new birth*

The human nature of a child is fallen. The children are as dead in trespasses and sins as the oldest and hardest of sinners. It is of no value to teach them a moral code or to urge them to love God, or simply that the sum total of Christianity is learning to be polite and respectable. The Sunday School teacher has no commission to train up a new generation of Pharisees. The natural child is dead in trespasses and sins and is bound for a lost eternity unless he is born again (John 3:1-8). The teacher must be much in prayer for this work of God to be done by the Holy Spirit, who alone can accomplish it.

3. *Conviction of sin*

Salvation must never be presented to children in terms which eliminate the child's sense of need. It must never be that we can 'give our hearts to Jesus'. That assumes that our hearts are of value, that they are pure enough and acceptable to Jesus. No, Jesus does not need our hearts, but our hearts need him. This goes for the child, too. Every child must become conscious of his need of Christ and this means becoming conscious of his or her own sin. What is salvation, anyway? Salvation from what? Christian salvation is always salvation from the condemnation which is due to our sins. This has to be handled delicately with children but must not be omitted. The teacher must spend time, therefore, in showing the child what sin is. This must be done in terms which the children will readily recognize. Children are not humanists by nature. They do not pretend to be basically good. They are ready to acknowledge the wrong that is within them far more readily than many adults. This wrong has to be shown for what it is, that is, sin. Sin is a coming short of God's standard, a going aside from God's way and conviction of sin involves a recognition of what we are in terms of selfishness, hatefulness and rebellion. Only the Holy Spirit can convict of sin (John 16:7-11), but he chooses to do so as the teacher employs the Scriptures to show how evil sin really is. Do not let the children grow up without knowing what the Bible says about sin – their sin. There is no such thing as salvation apart from repentance for sin.

4. The death of Christ

The substitutionary death of Christ must be taught. Again children are usually very ready to accept the concept of punishment. A wrong deserves to be punished. They do not have the objections of many adults to the idea of 'retribution' – attitudes which are often developed to cover sin from oneself. Moreover they are very quick to accept that it is a noble thing when one person willingly takes the blame to protect another. The uncluttered mind of the child seems to see these things so clearly. The New Testament teaches that Christ died in the place of the sinner to bear the penalty in his stead (Mark 10:45; Isa. 53:4-6; Gal. 2:20; 1 Peter 2:24). This truth is well expressed in a number of hymns suitable for children. The following are good examples:

We may not know, we cannot tell
What pains he had to bear;
But we believe it was for us
He hung and suffered there.

He died that we might be forgiven,
He died to make us good,
That we might go at last to heaven,
Saved by his precious blood.

There was no other good enough
To pay the price of sin;
He only could unlock the gate
Of heaven, and let us in.

Or the following:

And so he died! And this is why
He came to be a man and die:
The Bible says he came from heaven
That we might have our sins forgiven.

He knew how wicked man had been,
And knew that God must punish sin;
So, out of pity, Jesus said,
He'd bear the punishment instead.

The teacher will discover a number of illustrations of this truth, but they should be used with caution because none of them is capable of conveying the truth perfectly. The best illustrations must be the biblical ones. The two which come most readily to mind will be found in the story of the Passover (Exod. 12) and the account of Abraham offering to God the ram caught in the thicket, in place of his son Isaac (Gen. 22). There are many other biblical illustrations.

5. Receiving salvation

It cannot be stressed too much that to force children to repeat certain well-known stock phrases, as a means of pressurizing them into becoming Christians, is a gross violation of the privilege afforded to the Sunday School teacher. To abuse the weak mind of a child, or to invade the child's individuality, or to endeavour to subject his will to a mechanical process are to deny the need for the work of the Spirit of God. The teacher must not 'play God'. To do so will bring only a false profession, guarantee a falling away and possibly place a stumbling-block in the way of that person for the rest of his life. Every teacher should read carefully the Lord's severe warning against doing any such thing: 'But if anyone causes one of these little ones who believe in me to sin, it would be better for him to have a large millstone hung around his neck and to be drowned in the depths of the sea,' (Matt. 18:6). In any case, the idea that children should 'give their hearts to Jesus' or simply 'give their lives to God' is less than the gospel. Salvation is not by works, not even the apparently virtuous work of giving something worthy to God, like 'my heart' or 'my whole life'. We can give nothing to God. Our lives and hearts are not worthy! They are dark, dead things until illuminated and made alive by the Spirit (Eph. 2:1-9).

Salvation is by grace alone. It is the gift of God. A man receives salvation only through faith. God's Holy Spirit convicts of sin, leads to Christ and enables the sinner to believe in him. Faith, to be faith, must be a persuasion of the truth of God's Word. I must believe that I am a hopeless sinner, that Christ has died to save me and that God will save me if I trust in what he has done for me through his Son upon the cross. It is not a case of my heart being given to Christ (although that does follow), but rather of believing the promise of God, trusting myself to him wholly and accordingly receiving Christ into my heart and life.

The role of the teacher in all this is most delicate. Some unfortunate children who were delivered at birth by the use of forceps bear the marks of that intervention on the part of the doctor or midwife throughout their lives. How the teacher assists at the spiritual birth of a babe in Christ is a matter requiring great wisdom and much prayer. We must not force them. We do not want them to bear the marks of our intervention for the rest of their spiritual lives. Let the Word of God do its work (1 Peter 1:23). Let the Spirit of God do his work (John 3:8). The teacher must be alert, observant and ready to help and to encourage. The teacher ought to be ready to pray with a child who shows real understanding of his need and wants to be free from sin and sinful ways, expressing a desire to trust himself to the work of Christ upon the cross. Help such a child, but do not rush in. Leave the Spirit of God time and room to work. Do not put words into their mouths. Do not lead them in a step-by-step prayer. Listen to what they say. Thank God when they express themselves without the use of 'evangelical jargon'. Do not dismiss them because they have not used the 'right' words. Where the teacher believes that a real work of God is in progress then let him not only pray *with* the child but also earnestly *for* the child. Let the teacher be as wise and as gentle as our Lord himself, of whom it was said, 'A bruised reed he will not break, and a smouldering wick he will not snuff out . . .' (Matt. 12:20).

Dear teacher, or prospective teacher, have you read and digested this chapter? Please read it again, consult your Bible and learn the passages quoted.

For further study
Get hold of the following books, buy them or ask for them in your church or local library. They all contain helpful summaries of the major teachings of the Bible.

1. *The Shorter Catechism, with Scripture proofs* — Banner of Truth Trust
2. L. Berkhof, *Summary of Christian Doctrine,* Banner of Truth Trust
3. P. Jeffery, *Firm Foundations* — Evangelical Press of Wales
4. R.B. Kuiper, *The Bible Tells us So* — Banner of Truth Trust
5. J.I. Packer, *God's Words* — I.V.P.
6. J. Gresham Machen, *The New Testament — An introduction To Its Literature and History* — Banner of Truth Trust

(This last book is full of background information and is very useful for a study of the New Testament books).

Some useful whole Bible commentaries:
1. *The New Bible Commentary Revised,* I.V.P.
2. *Matthew Henry's Commentary on the Whole Bible,* Marshall Morgan & Scott.
3. Matthew Poole, *A Commentary on the Holy Bible,* Banner of Truth Trust.

Two Bible Dictionaries:
1. *The New Bible Dictionary*, IVP.
2. *The Lion Handbook to the Bible*, Lion.

1. v.11. See NIV Footnote; cf. Matt. 19:13-15.

13.
When?—Why Sunday?

While many churches still run the Sunday School at the usual time, others have transferred their main children's work to another time during the week. The reason for this is the well-known catalogue of practical difficulties surrounding the timing of the Sunday School. Sunday Schools were run on Sunday afternoons for many years with good attendances. However, with the post-war advent of *'le weekend'* and the proliferation of the motor car, Sunday afternoon attendances have dwindled seriously, especially the attendance of children whose parents are not church-goers. 'Throughout the Western world, attendance is falling so drastically that many forecast the demise of the Sunday School *in this decade*.'[1] Various alternative times have been tried for the Sunday School. Attempts to fit this in with the morning service are fraught with difficulties. If Sunday School is held before the morning service this means that the children of church-goers have a Sunday morning lesson lasting at least two hours, one in Sunday School and another in church with their parents. If, alternatively, the Sunday School is run concurrently with the morning service, then a considerable proportion of the congregation is regularly absent from the morning ministry of the church. The disadvantages of this have been discussed earlier, but the chief one can bear repetition at this point. It is that the Sunday School teacher, if he is to give out to the children, needs, perhaps more than anyone, to be taking in, and is the last person who ought to be regularly out of the Sunday morning service. Other radical approaches to the problem have been tried, such as 'all-age Sunday School', in which all age groups are taught separately and then meet together for corporate worship.

However, there is a much more radical, and in many ways more acceptable, alternative. Let us ask the question: 'Why do we have Sunday School on Sunday?' If we could once accept that our attempt to instruct children in the things of God should not be allied exclusively to the worship of the Lord's Day, then many other exciting possibilities open up. Why not a 'Wednesday' school or 'Friday' school? The separation of the main Sunday School work from the other activities on Sunday in this way does solve many of the problems surrounding the Sunday timetable – the traditional rushing about and the practical problems mentioned above.

Many Sunday Schools already hold a mid-week activities evening for the children of the Sunday School. This is run as a games or handwork evening and is intended to be a promotional aid for the Sunday School. It is very often a 'sprat to catch a mackerel'. Children may not come to the happy, enjoyable mid-week evening, unless they regularly attend the Sunday School, which in their eyes may be anything but a happy and enjoyable experience. This is certainly going to be the case if it is an alternative to a Sunday afternoon family activity, or involves them in a two-hour session on Sunday morning. These mid-week activities are frequently concluded by a brief time including a short talk and a closing prayer, with possibly the addition of some chorus singing.

. The idea of a 'Friday School' solves the Sunday problems and at the same time offers a meeting to which many children who have no church connections will be happy to come. It means that our approach to teaching the children, especially those of non-church-going parents, has to change from the context of 'school' to the context of 'club'. A well-structured evening can be planned with all the exciting and enjoyable activities of the mid-week evening. However, instead of a brief and somewhat lame epilogue, which is sometimes only tacked onto the end to remind children that it is 'church' after all, a full Sunday School teaching period can be included. All of the Sunday School teaching aids and materials can be used in this period, which may last for about half an hour. This is now the 'Sunday School', but not on Sunday.

An example of how this works is as follows. It is what actually happens in one 'Friday Club' which is held every Friday evening from 6.00–7.30 p.m. for the junior school age group.

> Opening time – 10–15 minutes
> Lessons in classes – 30 minutes
> Refreshments – 10 minutes
> Games and activities – 30 minutes
> Closing time 5–10 minutes

In the opening and closing times all the teachers and children meet together as they would in the first part of Sunday School. Here they review memory texts, sing choruses, are registered in classes and listen to any special announcements. This kind of programme means that all the teachers not only need to come prepared to teach their class, but also to run group activities, which can include team games, table games, table tennis, billiards, darts, handwork groups and cooking. It is very useful to have a time like this in which, during handwork, for example, models, pictures or friezes in connection with the lesson can be produced. It also provides a time in which teachers and children can relate together on a friendly basis, working and playing together. If teachers in fact are already committed to a mid-week activities evening as well as Sunday School, then to combine the two in this way is certainly not asking for any greater commitment of time from them. In fact, many teachers would testify to their appreciation of more time with their own families on Sunday.

Now it may be that some will feel that this suggestion is outrageous. Sunday School should be held on Sunday and Sunday would not be Sunday without it. Moreover, not to have Sunday School on Sunday may be seen as an encouragement for children not to observe the Lord's Day as they should. This might be seen to be undermining what Christian parents endeavour to teach their children about the priority of worship on Sunday. In reply to such fears it may be said that it is one thing to undermine the observance of the Lord's Day, but quite another to raise a legitimate criticism about what might be called 'Sunday tradition'. Certainly the efforts of church-goers to impress upon the children of non-church-goers the merits of keeping Sunday as a special day have not proved very fruitful. After all, we can hardly expect children from non-Christian homes to show any interest in treating Sunday as Christians would like them to do. And what is the point? We are surely not concerned primarily to make children who have no church connections into mere church-goers. If we can teach them the gospel of Christ and, in God's mercy, see them converted, there will then be no problem in introducing them to Sunday worship.

If the alternative is to pursue a Sunday School in which less and less children of non-church-going parents attend, then we shall in fact accomplish neither. At any rate, there is nothing to prevent the local church from arranging something like a catechism class for its younger children in connection with the morning service. A catechism is likely to prove effective with children from Christian families but hardly with others. If the family can be encouraged to learn the catechism together, and a short time is allowed in the morning service for its use, then this can be a most useful means of storing spiritual truths and biblical verses in the minds and hearts of young and old alike. A small class of these children on a Sunday morning need only involve one or two adults who, if they work on a rota basis, need only miss the occasional morning service. With some such arrangement the local church can be seen not to be neglecting the children of its own families and at the same time will probably get a much greater response from other children in the area. Parents will usually make their own personal decision about the age at which their children should stay in for the sermon.

The mentality of children has changed. The 'club' approach is attractive to them now whereas the 'school' approach is much less attractive. But if their mentality has slightly changed, their availability has certainly done so. There are many children who are simply no longer available on a Sunday. The motor car and the family outing, to say nothing of the increasing use of Sunday for social and sports events, effectively take them out of the reach of the local church. We do need to rethink the position in radical terms. In fact, the very existence of Sunday School should teach us this. What was the origin of Sunday School? As we saw earlier, the Sunday School movement in England was originated by Robert Raikes in 1780. He was basically a reformer who believed that idleness, vice, ignorance and degradation, which led to crime and in those days often to the gallows, could be avoided through education. When his efforts among the adults in Gloucester Jail failed he turned his attention to the children on the basis that prevention would be better than cure. It need not concern us that his method was more philanthropic than Christian, and depended on a faith in education rather than conversion. The interesting factor for our present considerations is that Raikes tried to gather these children into a school on Sundays. This school was situated in Soot (or Sooty) Alley, which was where all the chimney sweeps of Gloucester lived and it was one of the worst slums of the city. Raikes stated that the purpose of such a school was 'to furnish opportunities of instruction to the children of the poorer part of the parish without interfering with any industry of the weekdays.' Raikes did his work in a Sunday School *because that was the only time the children were available.* He was a radical. If we are to be of the same spirit and to seek the same opportunities, we need to be equally radical. It may be that the day of the Sunday School is over. But if we have the same burden for the spiritual good of children that Raikes had for their moral welfare, we should be prepared to make ourselves available to them when they are available. As Christians we have to stop arranging our evangelistic activities, including those for children, at times when they suit us and our traditions, and begin an endeavour to meet the people, including the children, when and where they are available.

I hope therefore, that it will be seen that the use of the term 'Sunday School' throughout this book is merely a term of convenience which is easily recognizable. The principles and practical suggestions outlined in the book are just as applicable to a Sunday School as to an 'Any-day-of-the-week School'. We need to be imaginative and sensible in the application of the principles to our own particular situation. This book has been produced in the hope that evangelical Christians and churches may find the means of doing great good, by whatever means we can, to the children of our day, who are in great spiritual darkness.

1. Donald Howard, cited in the *Banner of Truth* magazine for June 1984.

Epilogue

Teacher, you have your children in Sunday School for one precious hour a week. Does that dismay or thrill you? This one hour must never be approached in a mechanical, tired and bored manner. Consider the following exhortation from C.H. Spurgeon: 'Sunday school teachers, cry unto God that you may attend your classes with a sincere desire to promote God's glory, leaning wholly on his strength. Do not be content with the ordinary routine, gathering your children there and sending them home again; but cry "Lord, give us the agony that a teacher ought to feel for his child's soul." Ask that you may go to the school with deep feelings, with throes of love over the children's hearts, that you may teach them with tearful eyes, groaning before heaven that you may be the means of their salvation and deliverance from death.'[1]

---

1. C.H. Spurgeon, *New Park Street Pulpit*, Banner of Truth Trust, Vol 15. p. 476.

Also available from
Evangelical Press

BIBLE CLASS COMMENTARIES

by Henry T. Mahan

For those who teach Bible classes in Sunday School, house groups, Christian unions or youth groups; for those who want help in their personal devotions but do not have the time to study the weightier commentaries; for the Christian who wants a straightforward presentation of the key facts and messages of the epistles; for those wanting a handy, quick and reliable explanation of a passage or verse - here is the help they need in this complete verse-by-verse explanation of all the New Testament epistles from Romans to Jude.

R. T. Kendall *(Westminster Chapel)*
"Every Bible teacher and Sunday School teacher will want these commentaries at their finger-tips. They are balanced, simple, clear and right to the point. I highly commend them."

GO TEACH
Sunday School Teaching Aids

GO TEACH

(Teacher's manual)

    Beginners (Ages 3-5)
    Primaries (Ages 5-8)
    Juniors (Ages 8-12)
    Young Teens (Ages 12 plus)

COME LEARN

(Take-home leaflets)

    Beginners
    Primaries
    Juniors
    Teen Search